SO-ART-921

# Contents

**Chapter 6 - On The Road** (continued)

**Chapter 7 - At Home On The Road**

**Chapter 8 - Care and Maintenance**

# INTRODUCTION

We have been enjoying the world of RVing since 1963. Experience and fellow RVers have taught us a great deal about making RVing easy and enjoyable. We have written this book in the hope you will benefit from our collective experiences.

We won't get technical, but you'll learn how to select an RV that will satisfy your personal interests, needs and budget.

You'll discover how your RV's water, electrical and sewer systems work and what you should do to maintain them.

You'll learn how to drive, back and level your RV, use its self-containment features and hook up to a campground's utility systems.

We include a section on equipping and furnishing your rig. You'll add more but this will get you started.

You'll pick up some ideas on packing your RV and we'll share a number of time saving tips for cooking, cleaning and doing laundry.

We also discuss traveling, locating overnight stops and selecting campsites.

You'll learn how extended RV travelers do their banking, receive mail and keep in touch with their friends and family while on the road.

You're going to join the millions of people who have learned how easy RVing can be.

Enjoy The Journey!

# Why Are We RVers?

RVing complements our lifestyle. We use our RV to satisfy our desire to travel.

We have seen the sun rise over Cape Cod and watched it set off the coast of Puerto Vallarta. We have traced the Oregon Trail and traveled the length of the Alaska Highway. We have ridden trolley cars in San Francisco, explored the French Quarter of New Orleans and attended the theater in New York City. And at the end of each day we have prepared meals in our own kitchen, showered in our own bathroom and slept in the familiar comfort of our own bed.

Our clothes travel in closets and drawers. Our toothbrushes hang in the bathroom medicine cabinet and our favorite foods are always available in the refrigerator.

We stay or go according to our mood.

If the opportunity for adventure arises, we're free to respond.

We travel if we choose, when we choose, and where we choose.

To us, the real adventure is not in the destination but the journey. We travel not to get somewhere but simply to go.

We enjoy the freedom of the road.

And our RV makes it possible.

# Chapter 1

## CHOOSING AN RV

### What Is An RV?

An RV is a vehicle, self-propelled or towed, that provides mobile living accommodations. Those accommodations can range from spartan to luxurious, depending upon the type and size of rig you choose.

RVs offer queen or king-sized beds, full baths, air conditioning, and thermostatically-controlled forced-air heat. Their kitchens may be equipped with refrigerators, freezers and microwave ovens. Televisions, VCRs, CD players and ice makers have become commonplace in today's RV.

All of these amenities may be enjoyed whether you are parked in the luxury of a full-service RV resort or the primitive surroundings of a National Park campground. This is made possible by the RV's "hookup" and self-containment features.

Hookups allow the RV to connect to and utilize a campground's or RV park's electric, water and sewer systems. Many RV parks provide cable television connections and some even offer telephone hookups. Once an RV is hooked up to a campground's utilities, it can remain in place indefinitely.

Self-containment features permit the RVer to enjoy all the amenities of the RV without the necessity of outside connections. Electricity is supplied by storage batteries or a generator. A propane tank provides the fuel for cooking and heating. Fresh water is supplied by an on-board water tank. Waste water is stored in the vehicle's holding tanks until a disposal station or RV park's sewer hookup becomes available.

Self-contained camping is limited only by the capacity of the RV's self-containment features.

Depending upon your choice of location, an RV can be a beach cottage, mountain cabin or desert condo. An RV may also serve as a tour bus, guest room or office.

An RV provides the mobile living accommodations; you determine how it will be used and where it will go

## Interests, Needs and Budget

The process of choosing an RV is really no different than selecting a personal transportation vehicle.

If you love to drive in the mountains with the wind in your hair, a convertible sports car may be the right vehicle for you. If you have young children and haul groceries, gardening supplies and a Saint Bernard dog, perhaps a van is your vehicle of choice.

The point is, just as you select a personal transportation vehicle to fit your lifestyle, so should you choose an RV to meet your interests, needs and budget.

Consider your interests first. The reason you are getting an RV, after all, is to pursue your interests. How will you use the RV, where will you go, what will you do?

Next, think about your needs. The RV will have to satisfy certain personal needs so you can pursue your interests. Who will be the usual occupants of the RV? What will they require in the way of sleeping, eating and bathroom accommodations? You'll want comfortable seating for everyone while traveling. And don't forget room to store clothing and personal gear such as photography equipment and golf clubs.

As you shop, determine the type of RV (camper, trailer, motorhome, etc.) and features (self-containment, generator, air conditioning) that will best satisfy your interests and needs.

Paying attention to the prices will give you an idea of the type and size RV that will suit your pocketbook. The amount of money you'll spend on an RV will depend upon your budget. The purchase cost of the RV will include the final price of the vehicle with any optional equipment plus sales tax, registration, and possibly some miscellaneous charges or fees. The dealer will convert this into an affordable down payment and easy monthly payments (for as long as 15 years).

Ongoing expenses associated with owning an RV include the annual registration fee, storage fees, insurance, maintenance and repair costs.

Over-the-road expenses will include fuel, tolls, propane, overnight accommodations, groceries and laundry expenses.

## How People Use RVs

How will you use your RV? Where will you go? What will you be doing? The answers to these questions should influence the type and size RV you buy.

Look for an RV that will permit you to comfortably pursue your choice of RV lifestyle.

Recreational vehicles lend themselves to a variety of activities and lifestyles.

**Day trips** to the beach, mountains or desert are easily made in a camper, van or motorhome. There is comfortable seating enroute and the convenience of your own eating and bathroom facilities when you reach your destination.

**Weekend getaways and periodic vacations** are probably the most popular uses for RVs. Most vacation and travel destinations offer RV parks or campgrounds. Some RVers travel to one location and stay until it's time to return home. Others prefer to travel from one spot to another. Lounging at the beach, golfing in the desert or sightseeing in a city are typical RV weekend and vacation activities.

**Extended RV travelers** may be on the road for two or three months at a stretch. Their RV becomes a home away from home. They tour the country at their leisure, enjoying the scenery, and staying as long as they wish at destinations that interest them. While most extended travelers are retired couples, many are folks who have taken a temporary leave from their jobs or careers to satisfy a dream.

**Snowbirds** typically live in the northern regions that experience cold winter weather. They simply close up their homes for the winter and head south in their homes on wheels. Some return to the same RV park year after year. Others take advantage of the mild winter months to explore various southern states or Central American countries. A switch on this are the RVers who live in the southern regions and escape the summer heat by going north.

**Fulltimers** number in the tens of thousands (they don't stay in one place long enough for an accurate count). These RVers have made the move from their conventional lives and homes into their RVs and life on the road.

Some earn money as they travel, others have sold their homes and belongings and live on the earnings of their investments. Their "permanent address" is frequently nothing more than the address of a mail-forwarding service.

Eventually, most fulltimers return to a conventional residence, but they bring with them exciting memories of the places they've been and the things they've done.

## Where RVers Stay

RVs provide a lot of flexibility for overnight accommodations. As an RVer, you might spend one night in the convenience of a friend's driveway and the next night in the luxury of an RV resort.

An RV park and campground directory will provide you with the location, description, cost and even a rating of the RV parks and campgrounds throughout the United States and Canada. The RV you choose and its features should reflect the type of overnight accommodations you expect to utilize most frequently.

**Boondocking** means staying overnight in a spot that is not officially designated as a campsite. Roadside rest areas, truck stops, parking lots and friends' driveways are examples of boondocking sites. Laws must be obeyed, permission sought and common sense utilized when boondocking. The price for boondocking is usually free and the amenities frequently reflect the price. An RV's self-containment features will be important when boondocking.

**Government campgrounds** are generally located in scenic natural areas. Most provide a roomy campsite on reasonably level ground with a picnic table and firepit. Government campgrounds usually have restrooms, some with showers, a source of safe drinking water and a waste-water disposal station. A number of government campgrounds offer hookups. The cost of an overnight stay is comparatively modest but will depend upon the demand for the campground and the amenities available.

Since most government campgrounds were originally developed for tent camping, their campsites frequently are limited as to the size of RV they can accommodate. Some have established maximum length limitations at 24 to 28 feet. Others may have a limited number of sites that will accommodate RVs with lengths of 28 feet or more. Check with the campground or a campground directory for size restrictions.

**Commercial campgrounds** frequently offer more amenities than government campgrounds. Sites will be graded or paved and may include utility hookups. Restrooms should be modern with showers. Commercial campgrounds usually have a small convenience store and recreation facilities such as a swimming pool and playground. Dump stations and coin-operated laundry machines have become fairly standard features at commercial campgrounds. Obviously, the cost will exceed that of a government campground and will reflect its amenities as well as supply and demand.

Many commercial campgrounds try to appeal to tenters as well as RVers. Some originated as tenting locations and, like government campgrounds, a few may have length restrictions.

**RV parks** are planned and developed with the RVer in mind. Sites are level and often paved. Full utility hookups are usually offered at every site. Amenities typically include a convenience store, laundromat, modern restrooms with showers, recreation or game rooms, swimming pools and playgrounds.

RV parks may be conveniently located near main highways and designated as enroute parks. Destination parks are typically located where they can provide access to cities, recreation areas or scenic attractions.

**RV resorts** are RV parks with luxurious appointments and amenities. Lush landscaping, tennis courts and golf courses are frequently found at RV resorts. A number of resort hotels are beginning to include RV parks as a part of their facilities. Guests enjoy the same privileges as guests of the hotel.

RV parks and resorts rarely have size or length limitations but they may limit the use of their facilities to trailers and motorhomes.

Cost to stay at an RV park or resort ranges from moderate to expensive and could vary depending upon the time of year.

**Reservations** may be necessary at government and commercial campgrounds or RV parks and RV resorts just as they are at motels and hotels. Location, time of year and popularity all play a role in determining how soon the "No Vacancy" sign goes up. A campground directory will indicate if reservations are recommended and will provide a telephone number for further information.

We minimize the need for reservations by being "contrarians". We prefer to travel during the "off-season" months. May and October, for example, offer pleasant weather and uncrowded campgrounds.

## Types Of RVs

There are essentially two categories of RVs, towed and self-propelled. Trailers are towed; motorhomes, van campers and truck campers are self propelled. Each has its own distinct advantages and considerations.

### Towed RVs

The ability to separate a trailer from its tow vehicle affords a number of advantages. After arriving at a travel destination and unhitching the trailer, the tow vehicle is available for sightseeing or running errands. If engine problems require an overnight stay in a repair shop, the trailer and its occupants may remain in an RV park or campground. The tow vehicle can provide family transportation between trips. And, finally, the trailer or tow vehicle can be replaced or upgraded separately.

A trailer is going to require a properly equipped tow vehicle capable of handling the trailer (Refer to the sections, "Tow Vehicles" and "Trailer Hitches").

**Folding Trailers** (tent trailers) no doubt began as simple box trailers with a folding tent attached. The roofs and walls of today's folding trailers may be solid or fabric material. They may fold, hinge or telescope into place. The amenities may be as basic as a tent camper or as luxurious as an expensive motorhome. Many, and in some cases all, of the hookup and self-containment features can be found on camping trailers.

Generally, a folding trailer can be found to match the towing capabilities of most cars and trucks, even the small imports.

The greatest advantage of a folding trailer is economy. They are usually priced lower than other types of RVs. The cost of the hitch and electrical connections will also be relatively modest.

Folding trailers also have minimal effect on the tow vehicle's mileage and hill climbing abilities. They are easy to maneuver into tight camping sites and many are light enough to unhitch and move by hand. Lightweight boats can be carried on the trailer's roof while traveling. Folding trailers can also be stored in the garage between trips.

The folding trailer has to be set up before it can be used and taken down before it can travel. This can be inconvenient in foul weather. Daily setup and takedown can become a real chore when traveling every day. Items stored inside the folding trailer such as food, jackets and tools may be inaccessible while traveling.

Budget-minded couples will find the folding trailer a great way to begin their RV adventures.

**Vacation Trailers** (approximately 13 to 22 feet in length) are designed for versatility and economy of space. Couches and/or dinettes may do double duty as sleeping accommodations. They may or may not have a bathroom but will usually have self-containment features and hookup capability. Their size permits them to be towed to primitive campsites that may be inaccessible to larger RVs.

The vacation trailer can be towed by almost any properly equipped intermediate-to-full size car or truck.

This type trailer will generally satisfy the needs of the family who wants an RV for weekend getaways and occasional vacations.

**Travel Trailers** (23 to 40 feet in length) will have full hookup and self-containment features. The longer trailers provide more living and storage space. Sleeping accommodations will usually include a permanent bed or beds as well as the fold-out arrangements found in smaller trailers. Most bathrooms will come equipped with sink, toilet, shower and perhaps a small tub.

Trailers of this size will require a properly equipped full-size car or pickup truck as a tow vehicle.

**A conventional trailer's** front end (tongue) rides on a hitch located just to the rear of the tow vehicle's back bumper. This hitching arrangement gives the trailer owner the advantage of choosing a sedan, van, sport utility vehicle or pickup truck as a tow vehicle.

The travel trailer can be used for weekend trips, brief vacations or extensive travel.

**Fifth-Wheel Trailers** provide the same features found in conventional trailers of similar length.

The front end of a fifth-wheel trailer rides on a hitch that is positioned above and slightly forward of the rear axle of a pickup truck. The pivot point of this hitch arrangement results in a stable towing combination.

Hitching up to the trailer is simplified because the driver of the truck, looking through the rear window, can see both the trailer pin and the hitch receiver.

Since approximately four feet of the fifth-wheel rides in the bed of the pickup truck, the combined length of a fifth-wheel and its tow vehicle will be four feet shorter than the combined length of the same size conventional trailer and tow vehicle.

A properly equipped pickup truck is required to tow a fifth-wheel trailer. Approximately 20% of the trailer's weight is carried in the bed of the tow vehicle. The heavy truck suspension needed to support the hitch weight of this trailer may result in a hard ride when the trailer is absent.

**Self-propelled RVs**

The greatest advantage of a self-propelled RV is the comfort and convenience it provides on the road. While the seatbelts of the driver and passengers must remain securely fastened, they still enjoy the comfort of traveling in their living room. Passengers have the added benefit of being able to enjoy the entertainment center with its remote-controlled TV and VCR as the RV moves down the road.

Upon arriving at its destination a self-propelled RV does not have to be unhitched. This is a distinct advantage during inclement weather.

A self-propelled RV, because it is shorter than a trailer rig and doesn't bend in the middle, is considered by many to be easier to drive and maneuver. It can tow an economical tag-along car for destination use or a boat, horse or equipment trailer.

Van and truck campers are typically used for family transportation between trips. Motorhomes, though, usually remain in storage.

**Pickup Camper** units ride in the beds of pickup trucks. They can have the same amenities as a travel trailer depending on the size of the camper unit. Campers are designed for maximum use of available space and have the bed located above the cab of the truck. The camper unit can be removed from the truck but most owners prefer to leave it attached.

The compactness of the pickup camper allows it to be taken to primitive back road locations. Motorcycles can be attached to the front and/or rear of the truck. Boats or other trailerable items may be towed by a pickup carrying a camper.

The compressed living area of a pickup camper can be a disadvantage to those with large families or who wish to take extended trips.

It is important that the pickup truck be properly equipped to handle the anticipated combined weight of the camper unit, passengers and gear.

Be sure that the weight distribution of the camper is in accordance with the gross axle weight ratings of the pickup truck.

A distinct advantage of the pickup camper is the ability to use it as a second family transportation vehicle.

**Van Conversions** come in a variety of sizes and shapes. Some of the larger units are referred to as low-profile motorhomes. They offer a wide range of the features found in other RVs. Living space, like the truck camper, is compressed into a small area.

Versatility and ease of handling are the main advantages of a van conversion. They can be driven in congested city traffic and on back roads with relative ease. A van conversion can be used for commuting, family transportation, sightseeing, tailgate picnics and, properly equipped, as a tow vehicle for boats or travel trailers. A number of travelers combine camping in van campers with staying in hotels and motels.

**Motorhomes** offer the same features and amenities as travel trailers. They also provide easy passage between the driving compartment and the living area of the coach. This on-the-road accessibility of the motorhome's facilities is a significant reason for its popularity.

**Class A Motorhomes** are considered by many to offer the ultimate in RV luxury. The coach and driver's compartment are mounted as a unit upon the chassis of a heavy duty truck. They offer the same variety of features and amenities as travel trailers and fifth-wheels.

Larger Class A motorhomes, while comfortable on the road, can sometimes be difficult to maneuver in tight spaces and their size may exclude them from some government campgrounds.

Once established in an overnight site, it is inconvenient to use them for a quick trip to the store. As a result, many motorhome owners tow a small transportation vehicle during their travels (See Towing A Car).

**Class C Motorhomes** are sometimes referred to as mini motorhomes. The Class C's are the result of joining the chassis and driving compartment of a van truck with the coach of a motorhome.

A large bed or storage compartment occupies the cabover section. For those who may object to crawling into and out of a cabover bed, some longer models offer a separate bedroom. The efficient use of space and the familiar width of the driving compartment are desirable features to many.

**Micro-mini motorhomes,** smaller versions of the Class C, are mounted on the chassis and driver's compartment of small (usually imported) pickup trucks.

This smaller RV means a lower purchase price and reduced operating costs. Its size also enables it to be taken to more primitive campsites and to be used as a second family vehicle.

Care should be taken to avoid overloading the micro-minis because they frequently operate very close to their maximum weight carrying and drive-train performance capacities.

Obviously, each type of RV has its own unique advantages. It's not unusual for RVers to switch from towed to self-propelled and then back again as their needs and lifestyles change. Talk to owners of both towed and self-propelled RVs. Their reasons for choosing as they did will be food for thought.

## Size Of RVs

Choosing an RV usually involves compromising between mobility and living accommodations. Smaller RVs are more agile and fuel efficient while larger rigs offer more living comfort and amenities.

Road conditions and natural surroundings should be taken into consideration when choosing your RV. Narrow, twisting roads, overhanging tree branches and rocky outcroppings can make driving uncomfortable in extra-wide rigs. High-profile vehicles may be more susceptible to crosswinds and passing trucks.

Keep in mind that some government campgrounds and RV parks may have length limitations. Others may be unable to accommodate slide-out models. The more complete RV park and campground directories will list any size restrictions. Look up the types of campgrounds you plan to visit to see what size RVs they will accommodate.

You'll want to consider the number of people who will share the available living space and the amount of time they will be together in the RV. People might be good natured about putting up with a little less space and convenience for short periods of time. These minor inconveniences, though, can become serious aggravations during an extended journey.

Be sure to allow adequate room for the usual number of occupants to eat, sleep and store their personal belongings.

Generally speaking, the size, amenities and financial investment in an RV should be proportionate to the amount of time you will be traveling and/or living in it.

It's possible for a tent trailer to be used for full timing, but it is more appropriate for weekend trips and occasional vacations. Conversely, a 35-foot motorhome or large travel trailer can be used for just weekend trips but the financial investment seems a little out of proportion for such limited activity.

Look for a rig that is large enough to complement your present RV lifestyle and will allow you to sample or progress to another.

## Slide-out Rooms and Wide-bodies

**Slide-out** rooms on conventional trailers, fifth wheels and motorhomes have become increasingly popular. They provide more interior living space. At the press of a button, a section of the RV containing the couch, dinette, bedroom or a combination of these areas will expand up to three feet.

Slide-outs are particularly attractive to RVers who spend any length of time in one campground or RV park.

There are trade-offs, however. Units with slide-outs will cost more and add several hundred to a thousand pounds of weight to the vehicle. Depending upon its location, the slide-out room could add to a trailer's hitch weight and affect side-to-side weight distribution.

The slide-out mechanism reduces the amount of exterior storage space and the interior dimensions of the slideout room's overhead cabinets are often smaller.

Look for two sets of seals around the slide opening. One for the extended position and the other for retracted. You don't want dust, fumes and moisture leaking into the coach.

See if the seals "squeegee" the water from the walls and roof as the room retracts.

Seriously consider the benefits of equipping the RV with a "slide topper" or awning that keeps water, dirt and twigs from collecting on the roof of the slide-out.

Pay particularly close attention to the drive mechanism. If the drive system gets out of adjustment it can cause damage.

Ask the salesperson to demonstrate how the room is manually retracted if the drive mechanism fails to operate.

Be sure you test drive the unit. There shouldn't be any wind whistle, rattles or creaking while you are traveling.

While you are driving, see if the presence of the slide-out's wall behind the driver's seat is a distraction.

It may take more time for the heater to warm the interior of the RV and longer for the air conditioners to cool it down. Check to see if the insulation in the walls, ceiling and floor of the slide-out room is the same thickness as in the rest of the coach.

There may be a two inch difference between the levels of the coach and slide-out floors. Be sure the dining room chairs won't be perched precariously close to the floor's drop-off.

Do your homework. Compare the various makes and models. Ask owners of slide-outs what they would look for in their next RV.

*Tip:    Some RV parks are unable to accommodate slide-out rigs. You can get around this restriction by choosing a slide-out model that is functional with the room retracted.*

**Wide-body** is a term applied to RVs wider than 96 inches. Wide-body RVs may be as wide as 102 inches.

The extra width permits a greater variety of floorplans and adds to the spaciousness of the interior.

Wide-body owners should be aware that, while the maximum width limitation on most state highways is 102 inches, a few states still have width limitations of 96 inches.

## Diesel Or Gasoline?

Some RVs, because of their weight, can only be moved by a diesel engine. Manufacturers of large motorhomes, for example, may build their coach on a diesel equipped truck chassis and not offer a gasoline alternative.

The manufacturers of gasoline-powered pickup trucks place a limit on the amount of weight their product can tow. When the weight of the trailer exceeds that limit, the RVer has no choice but to buy a diesel-equipped truck.

Many motorhomes and towing combinations, however, offer a choice of gasoline or diesel engines. If you're seriously considering buying a diesel-powered RV, you should become familiar with the differences in the fuel, maintenance and operating characteristics of the diesel-equipped vehicle.

Here are some points to consider when deciding between gasoline and diesel-equipped vehicles.

The debate of gasoline versus diesel engines has gotten more lively as the manufacturers have improved their products.

A number of articles have been published comparing identical trucks and motorhomes equipped with diesel and gasoline engines.

The articles typically compare stock General Motors 454 and/or Ford 460 gasoline engines with a turbo-equipped Cummins 5.9 liter diesel engine.

Their comparisons indicate that given two identical RVs, one with a large gasoline engine and the other with a turbo-charged diesel engine, the performance of both vehicles is pretty close.

According to the articles, the RV with the gasoline engine will move away faster from a standing start but the diesel-powered rig will not be too far behind. Hill-climbing ability of the turbo-equipped diesel can equal or surpass the gasoline-fired rig. Once up to cruising speed, the performance of both vehicles is about the same.

A diesel engine adds to the vehicle's purchase price; $2,500 or more for a pickup truck and $20,000 or more for a motorhome. As a result, the resale price of the diesel rig will usually be higher than the gasoline-powered RV.

There is a significant difference in fuel consumption. In some published comparisons, the diesel-powered RV got up to 14 miles per gallon while the gasoline rig seldom achieved better than 10 miles per gallon.

Given these figures, if both these vehicles are driven 100,000 miles, the gasoline rig will consume 10,000 gallons of fuel and the diesel RV will burn 7,143 gallons. If gasoline and diesel both cost $1.35 per gallon, though, the gasoline-powered rig's fuel expense for the 100,000 miles would be only $3,857 more than the diesel rig's.

A diesel has fewer moving parts and fewer electronics so it has less maintenance, repair and breakdowns. Diesel repair and maintenance visits, however, are generally more expensive than those for gasoline-equipped RVs.

The diesel engine will reportedly provide more than 250,000 miles of use before requiring serious engine work. The gasoline engine, on the other hand, is usually due for overhaul at about 125,000 miles.

Diesel engines are noisier than gasoline engines. The diesel pusher, however, removes the noise from the driver's compartment to the rear of the RV.

The odor of diesel exhaust is objectionable to many.

Diesel fuel is less volatile than gasoline. The diesel fueling process, though, can be messy.

The diesel engine seems to be the choice of those who move heavy loads over long distances for extended periods of time. Its higher purchase price is offset by its longevity, lower repair costs over the life of the engine and higher resale value.

The gasoline engine, on the other hand, costs less to buy, does the job and its fuel economy is not far behind the diesel.

# RV Construction

A variety of construction techniques and materials are employed in the assembly of recreational vehicles. All in all, the popular brands offered by reputable manufacturers seem to hold together for years and years.

Motorhomes are mounted on a truck chassis. The chassis includes the frame, engine, transmission, drive shaft, axles, wheels, tires and suspension system. The motorhome manufacturer may alter the chassis by lengthening the frame, moving or installing a larger fuel tank or making other changes to allow construction of the final motorhome.

Most Class A motorhomes are constructed on a heavy truck chassis equipped with a large gasoline engine or diesel power plant. Class C motorhomes, on the other hand, are typically mounted on a cutaway van chassis.

If a motorhome is equipped with a diesel engine, it is usually mounted at the rear in order to remove the engine noise from the driving compartment. These models are known as diesel pushers.

Most trailer manufacturers mount their metal floor frames on leaf springs and one or two solid axles. Rubber torsion axles, said to offer a smoother ride, are becoming standard on some trailers. Mor/Ride suspension, available on the higher-end trailers, substitutes a configuration of rubber blocks for the leaf springs.

A number of methods are employed in constructing the living quarters or coach portion of an RV.

The coach may be framed with either wood, steel, aluminum or a combination of these materials.

Wood frames are usually 1 x 2's or 2 x 2's stapled or screwed together. High-end models may have screwed and glued joints. Lesser-priced units may simply be stapled together and rely on the surrounding sheathing for strength. Some coach manufacturers add a metal perimeter frame for strength. Interior paneling and exterior siding is stapled, glued or screwed to wood framing.

Metal frames are usually employed in laminated construction. Steel is claimed to be stronger. Aluminum is utilized for its light weight.

There are a variety of laminating processes. Basically they occur as follows:

The fiberglass outer skin is laid on a table and sprayed with adhesive. Thin wood paneling is placed on top of the fiberglass and it, too, is sprayed with adhesive. The prefabricated frame is laid upon the paneling and its open spaces filled with pre-cut block-foam insulation. This surface is sprayed with adhesive and covered by the interior wall paneling. The entire assembly is now pressed or vacuumed together.

The laminating process bonds the interior and exterior walls, framing and insulation, into a strong, rigid, yet lightweight wall.

Interior and exterior coach walls can also be screwed or riveted to metal frames.

There are manufacturers who cast the roof, walls and endcaps in fiberglass molds. Some cast the entire unit into one mold.

The coach may be insulated by attaching fiberglass blankets between the interior and exterior walls, placing polystyrene block foam between the frame members or spraying urethane foam that expands and adheres as it hardens.

Most RV manufacturers welcome visitors and conduct tours of their factories. We suggest you visit several factories employing a variety of assembly processes. The tour guides will be happy to tell you why their construction materials and methods are the best available.

There will always be lots of discussion and plenty of opinion as to which construction methods are best. All in all, the popular brands offered by reputable manufacturers seem to hold together for years and years.

## Vehicle Weights and Ratings

Before you buy any kind of RV be sure its cargo-carrying capacity and towing capability is adequate for your needs.

Manufacturers of car, truck, motorhome and trailer chassis rate their vehicles as being able to safely carry and/or tow a maximum amount of weight.

Overloading a chassis beyond the manufacturer's rating means exceeding the weight-handling capacities of either the tires, brakes, frame, transmission, engine or a combination of any of these.

Overloading an RV can also adversely affect its safe handling, performance, longevity and the manufacturer's warranty.

The purchaser of a motorhome or tow vehicle should determine the maximum amount of passenger and cargo weight that may be safety added to the vehicle and how much weight the motorhome or tow vehicle may safely tow.

The trailer buyer will want to know how much weight can be safely loaded into the trailer, how much the fully loaded trailer will weigh and how much weight the tongue of the trailer will place upon the hitch of the tow vehicle.

Essentially there are three weight categories: the weight of the vehicle before loading it with cargo and passengers (Unloaded Vehicle Weight); the weight of the vehicle after loading it with passengers and cargo (Gross Vehicle Weight); and the maximum fully-loaded weight allowed by the manufacturer's rating (Gross Vehicle Weight Rating).

Subtracting the vehicle's unloaded weight from the manufacturer's fully-loaded weight rating provides the amount of passenger and cargo weight that may be added to the vehicle.

Cargo and towing capacities of vehicles are usually expressed in the following terms:

**Tongue Weight** - the weight the coupler of a trailer places upon the ball of the tow vehicle's hitch.

**Gross Axle Weight** - the weight a single axle places upon the ground.

**Gross Axle Weight Rating** - the maximum weight the axle can safely place upon the ground as specified by the manufacturer.

**Unloaded Vehicle Weight** - the weight of the vehicle as built at the factory with full fuel tank(s), engine oil and coolants. The UVW does not include weight of fresh water, propane, the occupants (including the driver), personal belongings, food, tools, tongue weight of a towed vehicle, or dealer-installed accessories (such as awning, air-conditioning units, generator, hydraulic levelers, etc.).

**Gross Vehicle Weight** - the weight of the fully-loaded vehicle. This includes the vehicle, accessories, passengers, fuel, fluids and cargo. A trailer's Tongue Weight should be added to and included in the tow vehicle's Gross Vehicle Weight.

**Gross Vehicle Weight Rating** - established by the chassis manufacturer.  The maximum permissable Gross Vehicle Weight that can be handled by that vehicle's chassis.  This information is available on a plate or sticker attached to the vehicle.

**Net Carrying Capacity**  (sometimes referred to as Cargo Capacity) - determined by subtracting the Unloaded Vehicle Weight from the Gross Vehicle Weight Rating. It is the maximum amount of weight that may be added to the vehicle. This includes the driver, occupants, personal belongings, food, fresh water, propane, tongue weight of a towed vehicle and any dealer installed options or accessories.

**Gross Combined Weight** - determined by adding together the fully loaded weight of the tow vehicle and fully loaded weight of the trailer (or towed vehicle).

**Gross Combined Weight Rating** - established by the tow vehicle manufacturer.  It is the maximum total weight of the tow vehicle and trailer vehicle combination that may be handled by the tow vehicle.  This information should be available in the vehicle's literature or from the dealer or manufacturer.

**Tow Rating** - established by the tow vehicle manufacturer. It is the maximum weight of a fully loaded trailer that can be handled by the tow vehicle.  This information should be available in the tow vehicle's literature or from the dealer or manufacturer.

The RV buyer may want to look at a vehicle's cargo, passenger and towing weight capacities rather conservatively.

The maximum weight ratings established by the manufacturer indicate how much the equipment should be able to handle without failure. The ratings do not necessarily reflect how well the vehicle will perform when loaded to its maximum weight rating.

A towing combination loaded to its gross combined weight rating, for example, may have to creep over a steep grade in low gear. The same combination with 1,000 pounds less weight may top that grade very comfortably in second gear.

Look inside the RV for a label with the RV's weight information. It should contain the Gross Vehicle Weight Rating, the Unloaded Vehicle Weight and the Net Carrying Capacity.

Subtract, from the Net Carrying Capacity, the weight of any accessories (awnings, air conditioners, leveling jacks, etc.) that were added after the vehicle left the factory. Also subtract the weight of the LP gas that your propane tank(s) can carry. Finally, subtract the weight of the water you plan to carry as you travel down the road. (Refer to "Weights of RV Liquids" at the end of this section). You now have a fairly accurate picture of the amount of weight, including occupants, supplies and belongings, that may be safely added to the RV.

**Example:** A motorhome has a Gross Vehicle Weight Rating of 14,000 pounds. Its Unloaded Vehicle Weight is 12,000 pounds. What is the motorhome's Net Carrying Capacity?

| | |
|---|---|
| Gross Vehicle Weight Rating | 14,000 pounds |
| Unloaded Vehicle Weight | - 12,000 pounds |
| Net Carrying Capacity | = 2,000 pounds |

To that motorhome, the dealer has added two air-conditioning units (totaling 210 pounds), an awning (80 pounds) and a generator (260 pounds). The motorhome has a propane capacity of 20 gallons (85 pounds) and you determine that 30 gallons of water (250 pounds) is the minimum amount you wish to carry while traveling. How much passenger and cargo weight may be added?

| | |
|---|---|
| Net Carrying Capacity | 2,000 pounds |
| Accessories and Liquids | -  885 pounds |
| Passenger and Cargo Weight | 1,115 pounds |

**Example:**  The same motorhome has a Gross Combined Weight Rating of 19,000 pounds. If the fully-loaded motorhome weighs 14,000 pounds, what is the maximum Gross Vehicle Weight it may tow?

| | |
|---|---|
| Gross Combined Weight Rating | 19,000 pounds |
| Gross Vehicle Weight of the | |
| Motorhome | - 14,000 pounds |
| Maximum allowable weight of | |
| the fully-loaded towed vehicle | = 5,000 pounds |

**Example:**  A pickup truck has a Gross Vehicle Weight Rating of 8,500 pounds. Its Unloaded Vehicle Weight is 5,500 pounds. How much passenger and cargo weight may be added?

| | |
|---|---|
| Gross Vehicle Weight Rating | 8,500 pounds |
| Unloaded Vehicle Weight | - 5,500 pounds |
| Cargo Carrying Capacity | = 3,000 pounds |

**Example:**  The same pickup has a Gross Combined Weight Rating of 17,000 pounds. Fully loaded, it weights 8,500 pounds. What is the maximum Gross Vehicle Weight it may tow?

| | |
|---|---|
| Gross Combined Weight Rating | 17,000 |
| Gross Vehicle Weight of the Truck | -  8,500 pounds |
| Maximum Allowable weight of | |
| the fully-loaded towed vehicle | = 8,500 pounds |

**Example:** The same pickup has a manufacturer's Tow Rating of 8,500 pounds. Fully loaded, the truck weighs 6,000 pounds. What is the maximum Gross Vehicle Weight it may tow?

The tow vehicle should not pull a trailer that exceeds the manufacturer's Tow Rating, in this case 8,500 pounds.

An RV's weight (loaded or unloaded) can be checked at a public scale. Obtain a reading for each wheel and the trailer's tongue weight. If scales are not listed in your phone book, call moving van and storage companies or recycling centers. They may let you use their scale for a slight fee.

Be sure the cargo-carrying and/or towing capacity of the RV is more than adequate for your needs.

## Weights of RV Liquids

| | |
|---|---|
| Water | 8.33 pounds per gallon. |
| Propane | 4.24 pounds per gallon. |
| Gasoline | 6.3 pounds per gallon. |
| Diesel Fuel | 7 pounds per gallon. |

## Weight Distribution

The manner in which weight is distributed can affect the stability and safe handling of an RV.

Ideally, the weight should be distributed as equally as possible to each side of the vehicle.

A conventional trailer's hitch weight should be between 10% and 15% of its gross vehicle weight. A fifth wheel's hitch weight, however, may reach 25% of its gross vehicle weight.

The majority of the RV's weight should be placed above or in front of its rear axle. Too much weight pressing down on the rear overhang has a tendency to lift the front of the vehicle. This results in steering difficulties for motorhomes and stability problems with trailers.

If holding tanks are located behind the rear axle, try to travel with them empty. Any time the weight of the fuel, water or holding tanks (located behind the rear axle) is increased or moved rearward of the rear axle, its leverage effect lightens the load on the front of the vehicle.

Ideally, a trailer's water tank is located just in front of the rear axle. A 40-gallon water tank placed at the front end of a trailer could add or subtract up to 330 pounds to the hitch weight depending upon the amount of water it contains.

Consult the manufacturer's literature before mounting motorcycles, storage pods or other heavy objects on the front or rear bumpers of an RV.

Roof storage pods are best used for storage of lightweight objects to avoid raising the center of gravity. Besides, it's difficult to move heavy objects to and from the roof.

## Tow Vehicles

Choose and equip a tow vehicle so it is more than adequate to do the job. You won't regret the extra power, there will be less strain on the tow vehicle and less stress on the driver.

Selecting a car or truck as a tow vehicle requires a bit of research and thought.

First, decide what functions, in addition to pulling a trailer, the tow vehicle will be expected to perform.

What percentage of time will it be used for personal transportation and what percentage of time will it be used for towing? Consider how many passengers will be riding in the vehicle and for how long.

Decide whether a sedan, station wagon, van or pickup truck will best satisfy both your towing and personal needs.

It is important that the tow vehicle and towing equipment be properly matched with the fully-loaded weight of the trailer.

It you intend using your present car or truck as a tow vehicle, ascertain its tow rating, then buy a trailer whose gross vehicle weight rating is lower than your tow vehicle's tow rating.

If you are buying both a trailer and a tow vehicle, first locate the trailer that meets your interests and needs, then find a tow vehicle whose tow rating exceeds the trailer's gross vehicle weight rating.

New car, truck and trailer dealers should have the manufacturer's towing and weight literature. Compare the car or truck manufacturer's towing recommendations with the load that the fully loaded trailer and the towing circumstances will place upon the tow vehicle.

Since the towing recommendations will be expressed in weight, you may want to determine the following:

Tow Vehicle:

    Unloaded Vehicle Weight of the vehicle (fuel tank full)

    Anticipated Gross Vehicle Weight (fully loaded)

    Gross Vehicle Weight Rating

    Gross Combined Weight Rating

    Tow Rating

Trailer:

    Unloaded Vehicle Weight of the trailer

    Anticipated Gross Vehicle Weight.

    Gross Vehicle Weight Rating

    Hitch Weight

Assume, for the purposes of selecting a tow vehicle, that the trailer and the tow vehicle will be loaded to their gross vehicle weight ratings.

Many tow vehicle shoppers are faced with the dilemma of choosing between an engine that delivers fuel economy and one that delivers performance.

Fuel economy will certainly be very important if the tow vehicle will also be the primary transportation vehicle and will chalk up a lot of miles between towing chores. Only you can determine if the two or three miles per gallon difference will significantly affect your budget.

Engine and drive train performance will be a major consideration if you intend to tow a trailer in the western United States and Canada. Mountain passes in this region are frequently between 5,000 and 8,000 feet in elevation. A few exceed the 10,000 foot mark.

It has been determined that an engine loses about 3% of its power for every 1,000-foot rise in elevation. This means the engine will have 21% less power available while climbing a mountain pass at an elevation of 7,000 feet.

Keep in mind, while you may hear someone express a desire for improved fuel mileage, it's a rare occasion when an RVer, having reached the top of a mountain grade, kicks his tires and accuses his rig of having too much power.

Generally speaking, a tow vehicle with a long wheelbase and short rear overhang is the most desirable. This combination minimizes any side to side (sway) or up and down motion of the trailer's front end.

When the hitch is placed directly above or slightly in front of the tow vehicle's axle, as it is with a fifth-wheel trailer, the trailer has almost no side-to-side influence over the tow vehicle.

Earlier we mentioned buying a tow vehicle whose tow rating matched or exceeded the towing requirements of the trailer.

Usually, the tow vehicle can be purchased with the manufacturer's towing package. As the weight of the trailer approaches and exceeds 3,000 pounds, the towing package or factory installed options might include:

Heavy duty radiator

Engine oil cooler

Auxiliary transmission cooler

High-output alternator

Heavy duty suspension system

Stabilizer bar

Higher load-range tires

Hitch receiver

Electric brake controller

Wiring harness

Heavy duty turn signal flasher

Extended mirrors

In places where mountains and deserts will be encountered and when the trailer's weight exceeds 2,000 pounds, serious consideration should be given to equipping the tow vehicle with a weight distribution hitch, heavy duty cooling system and auxiliary transmission cooler.

Remember, safety considerations require that you refer to the manufacturer's towing and weight recommendations and consult both the trailer and tow vehicle dealers before making your final selection(s).

Choose and equip a tow vehicle so it is more than adequate to do the job. You won't regret the extra power, there'll be less stress on the tow vehicle and less stress on the driver, too.

## Trailer Hitches

When selecting a hitch be sure the manufacturers of the tow vehicle, trailer and hitch all agree on the compatibility and safety of the towing combination.

There are two basic types of trailer hitches, "Weight-Carrying" and "Weight-Distributing".

A **weight-carrying hitch** transmits the entire tongue weight of the trailer to the rear wheels of the tow vehicle.

A **weight-distributing hitch** applies the principle of leverage to distribute the trailer's tongue weight to all the wheels of both the tow vehicle and the trailer. A weight-distributing hitch would result in the tow vehicle carrying only two-thirds of the total tongue weight of the trailer. Trailers with a loaded weight exceeding 3,500 pounds a hitch weight exceeding 300 pounds require a weight-distributing hitch on the tow vehicle.

Hitches come in four classes:

Class I        Weight-Carrying, rated to 2,000 pounds of
               trailer weight.

Class II       Weight-Carrying, rated to 3,500 pounds
               of trailer weight.

Class III      Weight-Carrying or Weight Distributing,
               rated to 5,000 pounds.

Class IV       Weight-Distributing, rated to 10,000
               pounds.

Be sure the rating of the hitch exceeds the gross vehicle weight rating of the trailer. If possible, install a hitch with a rating that matches or even slightly exceeds the tow rating of the tow vehicle. On the other hand, mounting a Class IV hitch on a vehicle with a tow rating of 2,000 pounds wouldn't make much sense.

**Weight-distributing hitch spring bars** are rated for various hitch weights. If the trailer's hitch weight comes close to the maximum rating on the spring bar, it's safer to step up to the next higher capacity spring bar.

**Sway controls** attach to the weight-distributing hitch and help the trailer resist side to side sway that may be brought on by passing trucks or gusts of wind. One sway control should be sufficient, but another may be added if desired. The importance of this piece of equipment cannot be emphasized strongly enough.

There is a weight-distributing hitch on the market that moves the pivot point of the hitch from the hitch ball to a point just behind the axle of the tow vehicle. This just about eliminates any side to side motion of the trailer affecting the tow vehicle.

Be sure the manufacturers of the tow vehicle, trailer and hitch all agree on the compatibility and safety of the towing combination.

## Towing A Car

Towing a small car or truck behind a motorhome provides the convenience of economical transportation when the day's destination is reached. Errands can be run and sightseeing enjoyed without disturbing the parked motorhome.

Towing a small transportation vehicle does not significantly impact the fuel economy of the motorhome and the vehicle may be used for personal transportation at home between RV trips.

There is, however, the expense of owning and maintaining the second vehicle. You can expect to be charged for the additional vehicle at toll booths and ferries. The extra length may also cause some driving limitations in crowded or congested areas.

Consult the motorhome manufacturer's towing recommendations before towing any vehicle. Towing a vehicle of 1,200 pounds or more may exceed the braking capabilities of some motorhomes. (A number of states require operable brakes on towed vehicles weighing 1,000 pounds or more.) It is important that you do not exceed the motorhome's gross combined weight rating, its tow rating or its hitch weight rating.

Most cars with an automatic transmission or front wheel drive should not be towed if the drive wheels will remain in contact with the road and turn the transmission. Refer to the car manufacturer's towing recommendations.

There are three ways to tow:

**Tow Dolly -** A tow dolly allows a car with an automatic transmission or front-wheel drive to be towed by placing the drive wheels on the dolly. Some tow dollies are equipped with electric brakes for added stopping power. Keep in mind the dolly will add to the gross combined vehicle weight the motorhome must handle. Most dollies are not designed to be backed with a car on board.

**Vehicle Trailer -** A flat-bed or vehicle trailer, like the dolly, permits towing a vehicle with an automatic transmission or front-wheel drive. The trailer may be equipped with brakes and can be backed with the vehicle on board. The trailer will have to be registered, though, and adds considerably to the gross combined weight. You should also be aware that some campsites are not large enough to accommodate a motorhome, transportation car and a trailer.

**Four Wheels On The Ground -** Towing a car or truck with all four wheels on the ground is the simplest and most preferred arrangement. Some cars track better than others but if a car or truck has a towbar plate readily available for it, the car or truck probably has a history of towing satisfactorily.

After-market products permit vehicles with front-wheel drive and automatic transmissions to be towed with all four wheels on the ground.

"Lockout" devices may be added to the drive wheels of some front-wheel drive vehicles permitting them to free-wheel while being towed.

A transmission "uncoupler" installed on the driveshaft of a rear-wheel drive vehicle can separate the automatic transmission from the drive wheels while the vehicle is being towed.

Installing a transmission lubrication pump may also permit towing of a vehicle with automatic transmission or front-wheel drive.

Vehicles being towed with all four wheels on the ground should not be backed up. Backing could result in damage to the towed vehicle's steering components.

Remember, the manufacturers of the motorhome, towed vehicle and the towbar, dolly or vehicle trailer must all agree on the compatibility and safety of the towing combination.

## Self-containment Capacities

Determine how much self-containment capacity you will need, then compare the self-containment capabilities of RVs as you shop.

RVs are equipped with self-containment features which enable the occupants to enjoy the benefits of electricity, water, heat and refrigeration without being hooked up to a campground's utility systems. This is called "dry camping" by some, "boondocking" by others.

Most RVs are capable of providing two or three nights of self-contained comfort. That's more than enough for those who prefer the developed RV parks. Self-containment capacities may be more important, however, if you will be spending more than two or three days at a time in undeveloped or government campgrounds.

The RV's sales literature should list the capacities of its various self-containment features.

**12-Volt Battery** - An RV's interior lights, water pump, furnace fan, roof and stove-vent fans draw their power from the coach's 12-volt battery(s). The television, radio and tape deck may also receive their power from the coach's 12-volt system.

The capacity of a 12-volt battery is expressed in amp-hours. The small bulb in an RV's ceiling light draws about 1 amp of electricity. An 80 amp-hour battery, therefore, should theoretically provide enough energy to illuminate that light bulb for 80 hours. The higher the battery's amp-hour rating the longer it can go between recharging.

Most new RVs come equipped with a Group 24 deep-cycle battery. This battery has a rating of about 80 amp-hours. It should be adequate for a weekend of self-contained camping. A Group 27 deep-cycle battery, however, has a rated capacity of about 105 amp-hours or about 30% more capacity. Some RVs come equipped with more than one coach battery for additional amp-hour capacity.

Before installing additional batteries, you might want to see if the single coach battery isn't sufficient to meet your needs.

Be sure the coach is equipped with deep-cycle or marine batteries, not automotive starting batteries.

**Generator** (Also see "Options and Accessories") - The roof air-conditioner(s), microwave and other appliances requiring 120-volt household current will not operate on the coach's 12-volt electrical system. They are dependent upon either a campground's electrical hookups or a generator. A generator is usually an optional item and many RVs have an exterior cabinet that permits installation at a later time.

Be sure the generator is capable of providing for the electrical needs of the appliances. A roof air-conditioning unit, for example, will require about 2,000 watts of power and draw about 14 amps. Check the manufacturer's literature. Compare the generator's output with the demands of the appliances. Take into consideration that you may want to operate more than one appliance at a time.

**Propane Tank(s)** - Propane, also known as LPG (Liquified Petroleum Gas), provides fuel to operate the water heater, space heater, stove and oven. The RV's refrigerator is also capable of operating on propane gas. You'll use propane whether you have hookups or not. Figure on using about five gallons every two weeks. Having two propane tanks on a trailer is a convenience you won't regret.

**Water Tank** - Fresh water is carried in the RV's built-in water tank(s). A 12-volt pump delivers the water to the water heater, sinks, shower and toilet.

Experienced boondockers who practice water conservation boast about using two gallons per person per day. New RVers will probably use more. Estimate that you'll consume about five gallons of water per person per day. A 30 to 40-gallon fresh water tank is about average for most trailers and motorhomes.

**Holding Tanks** - Waste water and sewage is captured and retained by holding tanks until a dumping station or campground's sewer hookup is available. The sink and shower water flows into the gray-water holding tank; the toilet empties into the black-water holding tank.

Since the majority of the waste water will drain into the gray-water holding tank, look for a gray-water tank with a capacity close to that of the fresh-water tank.

## Options and Accessories

Decide which optional items you wish to include in the purchase price of your RV.

The options and accessories offered with RVs seem almost endless. Having the dealer include some of the more expensive ones in the RV's purchase price has a couple of advantages. Their purchase can become part of the negotiating process and, as part of the purchase price, they are included in the loan for the vehicle's purchase.

Here are some accessories you will probably want to add to your RV:

**Awning** - In addition to providing a shady place to sit outside, an awning shades one wall of the RV and helps keep it cooler. It can also shed rain, but care should be taken to prevent water from pooling on and damaging the awning. Fabric walls or screen material may be attached to the awning to create an enclosed room or an insect- free porch.

Be sure that when the awning is rolled into its traveling position, the upright arms will not prevent windows or exterior cupboards from opening.

You might also consider installing awnings to shade as many of the windows as possible. Glass can radiate an amazing amount of heat into an RV.

**High-powered, 12-volt, Roof Vent Fan** - Capable of three speeds and equipped with a forward or reverse switch, these fans will quickly remove hot air, condensation and tobacco smoke and draw in cool outside air.

**Air-Conditioner** - An air-conditioner will provide relief from the heat in both dry and humid climates. It requires 120-volt electrical power that is only available from a campground's hookup or the RV's generator.

Most RVers use their rigs during the summer months and consider an air-conditioning unit a necessity.

**Generator** - A number of electrical appliances require 120-volt electricity. These include the air-conditioner, microwave oven, electric coffee pot and hairdryer. An RV's generator can provide this electricity when electrical hookups are not available.

Generators come in a variety of sizes and capabilities. If you're going to spend the money for a generator, get one that provides sufficient wattage to operate one or both of your air-conditioners. Figure 2,000 watts for each roof air-conditioner. Add another 1,500 watts if you want to operate a microwave or hair dryer while the air-conditioner is running. Throw in another 500 to 1,000 watts for good measure and you're looking at a 6,500-watt generator.

A generator is an expensive item. Consider how often you will be without RV park hookups and still want 120-volt electric power.

**Hydraulic, Electric or Manual Levelers or Stabilizers** - These handy items are permanently mounted to the frame of the RV. Once parked, the RV is leveled and/or stabilized by simply turning a crank or pushing a button. Ask the dealer to demonstrate them for you.

Even with the levelers, it may still be necessary to occasionally place boards under one or more wheels to level the rig.

Motorhome owners will be able to operate the controls from inside and outside their rigs if the controls are conveniently located on the floor between the driver's seat and the driver's door.

**Backup Camera and Monitor** - It's almost impossible to keep an eye on that car you are towing behind your motorhome. The motorhome's side view mirrors are spaced so wide you look right past the towed vehicle. If your windshield mirror allows you to see through the rear window, it's so high you look over the top of the car.  A backup camera and monitor, however, are aimed right at the towee. Some systems even have microphones so you can monitor the sounds (or voices) at the rear of your RV.

**Television, VCR,  Radio and Tape Player** - These items are so common they are considered standard.  Check with the dealer to be sure.

**Citizens Band (CB) Radio -**    A very popular means of communication among RVers. This is especially true when two or more RVers are traveling together.  An inexpensive 40-channel model will do the job.  A good antenna is important. It's worth the money to have the radio and antenna professionally installed and tuned.

**Cellular Phone** - Consider a car-to-car or transportable model so the phone can be used in more than one vehicle and at home between trips.

## Shopping For An RV

Start by comparison shopping.   Look at motorhomes, conventional trailers, fifth wheels, pickup campers, van conversions and folding trailers.  Get an idea of the features, options and quality offered by the various types and manufacturers of RVs.

RV shows and RV dealerships are ideal places for comparison shopping.  Look at the expensive rigs first.  Notice the quality of the materials and workmanship that results in higher price tags.  Study the brochures of the rigs that appeal to you.

Determine whether you want a motorhome, trailer, pickup camper or van.  During the comparison shopping phase, you'll develop an idea of the type and size RV your budget will handle.

If possible, tour two or three RV factories. You'll gain tremendous insight into the different construction materials and assembly techniques.

**Floor Plans** - As you compare the variety of RVs, pay close attention to the various floor plans.

A bedroom that can be closed off from the rest of the RV provides privacy for changing clothes and accommodates occupants with different bedtime schedules. If you plan to spend long periods of time in your RV, you'll appreciate the ability to get away from each other occasionally.

Bunk beds are great space savers. Kids love them, but adults may find them awkward to get in and out of or, for some, too confining.

The location of the bathroom is an important consideration in selecting an RV.

A rear bath can be large and offer privacy. But if the only access is through the bedroom, guests sleeping in the front of the RV may disturb the occupants of the bedroom when they use the bathroom.

Center-side baths usually separate the bedroom from the rest of the RV. This bathroom, while it may be smaller, is accessible by the occupants of either the front or rear without disturbing each other's privacy.

A split-bath arrangement also separates the bedroom from the balance of the rig. It typically places the shower on one side of the aisle and the sink and commode on the other. Closing a door at each end of the bathroom creates a spacious bathroom area. Closing both doors also blocks travel between the bedroom and the rest of the RV.

Some split-bath floorplans put the sink and commode in an enclosed room across the aisle from the shower. This arrangement permits use of the sink or toilet without blocking the aisle yet still allows creation of a larger bathroom when showering.

Larger, more convenient kitchens may be found at the front or rear wall of the RV. Meal preparation in this location is not disturbed by traffic to and from the rest of the rig.

Many trailer owners have observed that the smoothest riding portion of the trailer is closest to the hitch. As a result, they prefer to have the kitchen and its breakables located forward of the rear axle.

Free-standing tables and chairs are homey and spacious. Bench seat dinettes, however, double as additional sleeping accommodations and usually have considerable storage space under the seats. Dinettes also provide seating (and seatbelts) for passengers in many motorhomes.

Couches offer comfortable seating (possibly with seatbelts), may convert to a bed and frequently have storage underneath.

**Specific Search -** At this point, review and update your list of interests and needs. Write a description of your ideal RV. Be as specific as possible. Write down the type of RV, size, engine, cargo capacity, sleeping, eating and storage accommodations, bathroom facilities, floorplan, self-containment capacities and accessories.

Begin the search for your ideal rig. Be flexible. Compromises will have to be made. Alter your written description as you look.

**Narrow the Focus -** Locate one RV that comes close to the written description of your ideal RV. Carry only that rig's brochure as you continue shopping.

When you find an RV that comes closer to what you are looking for, pick up its brochure and put away the previous one. (Keep your old brochures. You may want to refer to them).

Now locate an RV that comes even closer to what you're looking for than the one whose brochure is in your hand.

Keep repeating the process. This system will focus your search. Rather than comparing all the RVs with everything you've seen, you'll be comparing only two RVs with each other. And you're searching for only one RV that comes closer to what you are hoping to find.

## Evaluating Livability

Once you have narrowed your search to three or four RVs, you can start evaluating their livability.

The day-to-day livability of your RV is important. Before making a final decision, go through the RV and try it on for size.

If you are looking at self-propelled RVs, try on the driving compartment for comfort and convenience. Are the seats comfortable? You'll be spending a considerable amount of time in them. Are they accessible? The front passenger seat of some vans and motorhomes can be partially blocked by the engine compartment. Will this be a problem? Some Class A motorhomes do not have a driver's access door. Is this important to you? Is visibility for driving and sightseeing acceptable?

If you are looking at a slide-out model, is the bathroom accessible when the slide-out room is in the traveling mode? This could be important during a stop at a rest area. Some models permit complete and comfortable use of the RV in both the expanded and traveling mode.

Check the windows. Are there enough to provide adequate light, visibility and ventilation? Do they open? Sliding windows permit unrestricted visibility but must be closed against the rain. Torque-pane or jalousie windows hinge open from the bottom to admit air but prevent entry of rain. As you move about the coach, look for sharp corners on overhead cabinets that could obstruct your passage. They are often found above chairs and near doorways. See if there are adequate and accessible electrical outlets, especially in the kitchen and bathroom. Check the livability of each area, one at a time.

**Bedroom** - All the occupants should try on their sleeping accommodations. If two people are going to share a bed, both should lie down on it at the same time to determine if it is comfortable and large enough. Climb into the bed above the driving compartment of a pickup camper or Class C motorhome. Is it easily accessible? Can you turn over without bumping against the ceiling? Will the proximity of the ceiling and walls bother you? Island beds provide aisle space on both sides of the bed.

This allows easy access for bed making. It also eliminates the need for one occupant to climb over the other when getting in or out of bed. Locating one side of the bed against a wall, however, is space efficient and not a problem to most people. Do you intend to use form fitting-sheets? Measure the RV's mattress and compare it with the measurements of form-fitting sheets you can buy at the store.

Are the other beds of adequate size? Convertible dinettes and sofas are often rated as being able to sleep two. Most often they will only accommodate two children or one full-grown adult. Will the foldout bunk(s) support the size and weight of your child(ren)?

**Kitchen** - The kitchen, to many, is the most important area of the RV. Try it on carefully and see if it will fit your lifestyle.

Is there sufficient counter space to prepare a meal? If not, can you use the table or top of the range for an additional work area? Can an extension be added to the existing counter top?

Can you reach overhead cupboards? Is there enough storage area for your kitchen items? Are cupboards deep enough for dishes, pans and food? Is the kitchen floor covered with carpet or linoleum? Spills wipe up easier from linoleum. Does the kitchen have the features you want? Most RV refrigerators have sufficient capacity. Does the one you are looking at have a separate freezer compartment or will you have to open the refrigerator door to gain access to the freezer?

Microwave ovens are commonplace in many of today's RVs, and convection ovens may be offered as an option. Propane ovens used to be a standard feature in most RVs; however, there seems to be a trend nowadays toward offering the oven as an optional item. If you opt not to have the propane oven, you'll probably have a large storage cupboard in its place. Keep in mind, though, that microwave and convection ovens will be dependent upon electrical hookups or a generator whereas gas ovens are not.

Go through the motions of preparing a meal. Try the kitchen on. Does it fit?

**Washer/Dryer** - Many larger RVs offer a combination washer and dryer as an optional item. If this is a feature you are considering, keep in mind that, in most cases, you'll require water, sewer and electric hookups to operate a washer and dryer. You'll find that the capacity is smaller than you are used to at home, and it takes longer to go through its cycle. To many, the convenience far outweighs any negatives. Balance off the pros and cons. You may decide to opt for the large storage cupboard instead .

**Bathroom** - This is the area that can provide a lot of surprises. Go into the bathroom and shut the door. Go through the motions of getting dressed or undressed. Stand in the shower, close the curtain and go through the motions of bathing and washing your hair. Sit on the toilet, stand at the sink, reach into the cupboards and drawers. Be sure there's room to function. Is the toilet-paper holder convenient? Where are the electrical outlets? Where will you throw your trash, hang the towels, store the shampoo and soap?

An RV bathroom will not be as large as one in a house. Compromises will have to be made. Large or small, though, an RV bathroom should provide the same basic amenities as those in a house.

**Living Room Area** - Sit on the couch and chairs. Will they remain comfortable through a two or three-hour visit? Convert the couch into a bed. How many will it comfortably sleep? Will other furniture have to be moved? Where? Will the couch, converted to a bed, block the flow of traffic from one end of the RV to the other? If the rig doesn't have a lounge area, where will people spend evenings and rainy days? The dinette is the logical choice. Is it comfortable and is there room to sit, play games or visit?

**Storage** - Fulltimers will need storage facilities for all of their worldly goods. Extended travelers will have to bring clothing for a variety of activities and weather conditions. Vacationers may want to tote along sporting equipment. Some RVers will need room for fishing and hunting gear. Toys and games will have to be kept in a convenient spot for the kids. Exterior access to storage will be needed for leveling blocks, barbeques, camp chairs, tools, hoses and other equipment. Storage can be added, if necessary, by installing storage pods or racks on the roof.

## Previously Owned RVs

A used RV can be an excellent value. Purchase price, insurance and registration costs will be lower than for a new model.

Dealers frequently keep their best trade-ins and resell them with a limited warranty.

Look in the want ads; there are a lot of used RVs on the market. Drive through your neighborhood. How many RVs have been sitting unused in their driveways for long periods of time? Some people buy an RV and only use it once or twice a year. A used RV may have only a few thousand miles on the speedometer but, because of its chronological age, the price tag is half the original purchase price.

After determining that the used RV is in your price range and will satisfy your needs, notice if it shows pride of ownership. A carelessly treated living area may indicate the more critical areas have not been maintained either.

Look at the outside skin. Minor dings and scratches may be acceptable. Larger dents, especially on edges and corners, may be an indication of structural damage. Get down and check the undercarriage. The bottom of an RV can collide with rocks just as easily as the roof can run into tree branches and the walls into street signs. Bulging or stained ceilings or wall panels can mean a water leak and damaged structural members.

Examine each system one at a time. Look at the water tanks and the plumbing for signs of damage or leaks. Taste the water. Run water through every faucet. Check the water heater. Does it ignite easily? How long does it take to heat the water? Fill the holding tanks to check for leaks. Dump the holding tanks to check the operation of the dump valves.

Inspect the propane system for structural soundness. Operate each gas-fired appliance. This should include the range, oven, refrigerator, furnace and water heater. The flames should burn with a blue color; yellow flames indicate correction is needed.

The coach battery should be capable of being charged by the engine's alternator. Does the RV have a gauge that allows you to check the battery condition? Connect the RV to a source of household electricity. Check all the electric lights and outlets. Run the fans and furnace. Run the refrigerator on both 12 volt and household power (if it is designed to use these sources).

Take the RV for a test drive. Travel a variety of road conditions. Include curves, grades, traffic and highway speeds.

Have an RV service technician inspect the coach systems and provide an estimate of the cost for any needed repairs or adjustments.

Have a mechanic check the power train and brakes. This may cost a few dollars but it will be well worth it.

Compromises will have to be made. A used RV is not going to be in the same condition as a new one. Determine what it will cost to have the RV put into the condition you require. Add that to the purchase price to arrive at the true cost of the RV. Compare that cost to other RVs you have shopped. Ask your bank or credit union to tell you the "Blue Book" price on that model of RV. Having gathered this information you should be able to establish the maximum purchase price you are willing to pay for that particular RV.

Ask for all the instruction manuals that came with the original equipment.

*Tip: Ask to see the repair and maintenance records. They are a good indication of pride of ownership and will be helpful when future repairs are made.*

## Final Research

Talk to other RVers. You'll find them in campgrounds, RV parks and RV accessory stores. Ask about their rigs, their dealers and their experiences with getting their RVs serviced. Tell them you are about to purchase an RV and ask if they have any advice for you. You'll be amazed at the helpful feedback you'll get.

Research the RV manufacturer. How long have they been in business? How much longer will they remain in business? What kind of reputation for after-market support does the manufacturer enjoy? Ask owners of that manufacturer's RVs if they would buy another.

Research the dealer. His name will be on the license plate frames of the rigs he's sold. Ask the RV owner if he would do business with that dealer again. Ask if he is satisfied with the dealer's service department. What kind of reputation for after-market support does the dealer have? Visit the dealer's service department. After you buy your RV, your dealings with the sales person will end and your relationship with the service department will begin. Would you want to take your RV there for warranty work and repairs?

By the way, before going out of town to buy an RV for a little less money, keep in mind where you will go when your RV needs attention. Who do you think your hometown dealer will give preferential treatment to, the individual who purchased from another dealer or his own customer?

## Emotions

Through all of the list making, analysis and shopping, keep in mind your new RV is going to be your home away from home. You want to feel comfortable in it. Your RV will be a reflection of who you are. You'll want to show it off and be proud of it. Find a rig you can fall in love with. You'll take better care of it and enjoy your journeys that much more. Just be sure to fall in love with an RV that will satisfy your interests, needs and budget.

# Chapter 2

## GETTING TO KNOW YOUR RV

It's exciting! You've just brought that new RV home. You can't wait to load up the groceries and hit the road. But, wait a minute. Do you know how to operate all those appliances? Does everything work as it should?

Let's face it, the first night in a campground with a new RV is not the time to learn how to operate the forced air-furnace or to discover a leak in the fresh water system.

One of the keys to successful RVing is being comfortable with driving and operating your rig. To acquire that confidence, take the time to get thoroughly acquainted with your RV before you make that first journey.

There are three phases to getting acquainted with your RV: The dealer walk-through, familiarization at home and the shakedown trip.

### Taking Delivery

When you first take delivery of your RV, expect the dealer, a salesperson or a technician to spend a considerable amount of time with you. They will introduce you to the rig, its systems and appliances. This is frequently referred to as a walk-through.

Folding tent trailer buyers should be shown how to set up and take down their rigs.

Novice trailerists should see a hitching, backing and unhitching demonstration.

New motorhome owners should learn how to operate those levelers.

All of these procedures should be repeated under the watchful eye of the instructor.

You will be given a lot of information in a relatively short period of time. Don't expect to remember it all. Be prepared to take lots of notes. Better yet, make a tape recording of the entire process. Some buyers have even been known to video-tape the instructions and demonstrations. Take advantage of this opportunity to ask questions.

The dealer should also provide you with the manufacturer's warranties and instruction booklets for the RV, its appliances and other equipment.

If you are purchasing the RV from a private party, be sure the seller is willing to provide all of these demonstrations. Ask the seller for the instruction manuals he received with the RV; and, if possible, obtain the vehicle's repair and maintenance records.

Before you leave, ask for a telephone number you can call if you have any questions.

## Familiarization At Home

Set aside a day at home to get acquainted with your RV. You want to learn where things are located, how to operate them and to determine if they are working properly.

Keep pen and paper handy. Make a list of any questions you may have for your dealer or service technician.

Thoroughly inspect your RV. Systematically, inside and out, explore every cupboard, nook and cranny. Pay close attention to the location of the plumbing and wiring inside the cupboards.

Read through all of the instructions. Then, one at a time, read the instructions again and operate each system, appliance and piece of equipment. The objective, at this point, is to learn how to work everything and to check its operation.

Connect the RV's water hose to a faucet outside your house. Run water through all the RV faucets. Check the plumbing inside the empty cabinets and under the rig to be sure there are no water leaks.

Plug the RV's electrical cord into an electrical outlet in your house. You may have to use an extension cord and an adapter. Check the RV's lights, appliances and electrical outlets one at a time. Chances are the 20-amp electrical outlet in your house will not provide adequate current to operate the roof air conditioner properly. Wait until you are connected to a 30-amp outlet in a campground.

Turn on the propane at the tank. Switch on the propane leak detector. Following the manufacturer's instructions, operate each of the gas appliances one at a time. Propane appliances may take a few moments to ignite if they haven't been used for some time. Light the stove-top burners one at a time. Next, turn the oven on. The water heater is next, then the furnace. It's normal for a forced air furnace, after ignition, to take a minute or two to activate the fan. Finally, switch the refrigerator to propane operation, turn it on and give it about 12 hours to reach operating temperature.

Practice operating the leveling jacks, slide-out rooms, awnings, folding antennas and other accessories.

Disconnect the water hose and unplug the electrical hookup cord. Now operate all the RV's systems and appliances in the self-contained mode.

Double check the instructions as you operate each appliance or piece of equipment.

Start the RV's generator if you have one. Let it run for a minute or two before operating any of the RV's electrical appliances. Run the air conditioner(s). Before shutting down the generator, allow it to run for a few minutes after all the electrical appliances have been turned off. Now is the time to become familiar with the underside of your rig. Check the ground first. A puddle of oil or water under your rig may indicate a problem. Look at the bottom of the radiator, engine and transmission. There shouldn't be any water under the radiator. There should be little, if any, oil on the bottom of the engine and transmission oil pans. Look at the tires for signs of damage or unusual wear. Take a long look at the rest of the undercarriage just to see what it looks like. Performing this inspection at the beginning of each travel day will give you the opportunity to spot any unusual changes.

Become familiar with your rig's driving characteristics. First, take some time to properly adjust your rear and side-view mirrors. Sit in the driver's seat and, looking in the mirrors, determine the location of your "blind spots". These are the areas to the rear and sides of your rig that you can't see when you look in your mirrors.

Knowing your RV's dimensions will give you a sense of confidence as you approach low bridges, tunnels and gas station overhangs. Measure the distance from the ground to the uppermost part of your RV. This could be the top of the air conditioner shroud or the storage pod. Next, measure the distance from the ground to the top of the rig's highest antenna. Then, measure the width of the RV to the outside edges of the mirrors. Note the measurements on a card. Post the card on the dash or visor where the driver can quickly refer to it.

Drive the RV around your neighborhood. Locate a large empty parking lot and practice backing and turning. Cardboard boxes and/or one-gallon plastic bottles can be placed to simulate curbs, lanes and obstacles. A little water or sand in the bottles will keep them from blowing away. Test your brakes and stopping distances. When you feel ready, take the RV into traffic and out on the open highway.

Once you've gained some confidence in your ability to handle your RV, you are ready for the final and most important phase of getting acquainted with your RV: the shakedown trip.

## Shakedown Trip

The purpose of a shakedown trip is to detect any problems with your RV and get them corrected before you go out on the road for any length of time. Locate a nearby RV park or campground that offers 30-amp electrical, water, sewer and cable TV hookups. Plan on spending at least two nights in the campground.

Select a route to the RV park that includes traffic, hills and open highway. A variety of road conditions will provide an opportunity for you to become familiar with your rig's road-handling characteristics.

Begin the trip with full propane, water and fuel tanks. This will allow you to measure your consumption. Don't forget to bring all those instruction manuals.

Turn on the refrigerator and allow it to get cold before loading it with food. Whenever possible, put food that is already cold into the RV's refrigerator.

When you are ready to go, turn off any propane appliances and close the valve on the propane tank (the food in the refrigerator will stay cold for a long time). Close the windows and roof vents. Secure the cupboard, closet and refrigerator doors. Lower the TV antenna.

Make sure all hitch connections are secure. Check to see that the running, brake and signal lights are operating properly. Be sure the leveling jacks and door step are retracted before moving your rig.

It's a good idea to develop a departure routine. Forgetting to lock the refrigerator, lower the TV antenna or to raise the door step can be costly mistakes. Many RVers, knowing how important this can be, develop a departure checklist.

As you travel, keep a close watch on the temperature and oil pressure gauges. Halfway to your shakedown destination, pull off the road and do a visual check of the entire exterior and underside of the rig. Pay close attention to the hitch connections. When you reach the campground, repeat the inspection of the exterior, underside and hitch connections.

Park and level your rig in the campsite but do not connect to the electricity, water or sewer hookups. The best way to test all the self-containment features is to spend the first night using them. Turn on the propane and switch the refrigerator to propane operation.

The first day and evening, make a point to use all the self-containment features. Turn on the water pump. Run water through all the faucets. Operate the water heater, furnace, stove, oven, fans and all 12-volt appliances. Check all the interior and exterior lights. Don't overlook the lights in the exterior lockers.

Keep an eye on the monitor panel. Its gauges indicate the levels of the propane, water and holding tanks. It also shows the battery's state of charge. A rapid, unexplained change may indicate a problem.

Pay close attention to the operating temperature of the refrigerator. You may have to adjust the temperature a few times to find the right setting.

Experiment with the TV antenna to obtain the best reception.

Before going to bed look for water leaks inside the cupboards and under the RV.

Begin the second day of the shakedown trip by checking the battery, water, propane, and holding tank gauges. This will give you an indication of one day's self-containment usage.

The second day and evening should be used to check out the RV's hookup features.

Connect your RV to the campground's electrical, water, sewer and cable TV hookups. Once again, check for water leaks.

The black-water holding tank should have sufficient capacity to last through the third day. The gray-water tank, however, may be dumped at this point and its valve left open. This will allow the gray water to flow through the tank and into the RV park's sewer.

A better alternative would be to leave the valve closed and retain the gray water. It will then be available the next day to flush out the sewer hose after dumping the black-water tank.

Switch the refrigerator from propane to electrical operation. Continue monitoring the temperature.

Run all of the RV's electrical appliances including the air-conditioning unit(s). Check all the electrical outlets.

Operate the television on the campground's cable antenna and learn how to use the VCR.

Day two may also be a good opportunity to reorganize cupboards and make a list of the things you want to bring next time.

On day three, empty the holding tanks. Dump the black-water tank first and close its valve. Then dump the gray-water tank. The gray water will flush the black water out of the sewer hose. Double check to be sure both holding tank valves are closed after dumping.

Disconnect the hookups and check the monitor panel. The converter's battery charger should have returned the battery to full charge, the propane level should not have dropped more than about a half gallon, and the holding tanks should read empty.

Go through your departure routine or checklist before moving your RV from the campsite. Repeat the exterior and underside inspection about half-way home.

Make an appointment with your dealer or service center for any repairs or adjustments and to get your questions answered.

The dealer walk-through, home familiarization and shakedown trip will familiarize you with every inch of your RV and its operation. After the corrections are made, you'll feel confident that both you and your RV are ready for a long trip.

# Chapter 3

# RV SYSTEMS - HOW THEY WORK

The purpose of an RV is to provide mobile living accommodations. To accomplish this, the manufacturers have designed RVs with electricity, gas, water and sewer systems that will function wherever you park.

This means you can connect your RV to a campground's water, electricity and sewer systems while you are parked there.

Or you may park in a remote wilderness that has no utilities. Your RV's self-containment features will provide you with gas, electricity, water and waste-water storage capability.

A basic understanding of how your RV's gas, electricity, water and waste-water disposal systems work will make RVing easier for you.

All RVs (campers, trailers and motorhomes) use basically the same type of utility systems, appliances and accessories. Each brand or manufacturer, however, may be different. Be sure to read the manufacturer's instructions in conjunction with this book. The manufacturer's instructions are ultimately the ones to be followed. Contact your dealer or manufacturer if you have any questions.

## Electrical System

An RV's electrical system is a complex assemblage of wires, connections, contraptions and doo-dads. Some are mystified by it, a few may even be intimidated, but all of us take it for granted. Turn on a switch and it works!

You can live in harmony with your RV's electrical system by following the instructions supplied by the manufacturer. A basic understanding of how it works, though, can make RVing easier for you.

Here is a non-technical look at an RV's electrical system.

Essentially, an RV has three independent electrical systems:

1. The 12-Volt DC (Direct Current) automotive system.
2. The 12-Volt (Direct Current) coach system.
3. The 120-Volt AC (Alternating Current) system.

While the three systems are independent, they also interact with one another. Let's look at them one at a time.

**The 12-volt automotive system** provides electricity to operate the RV's engine, running lights, windshield wipers, horn and other automotive accessories.

Generally speaking, most of the electrically operated items controlled from the driver's seat belong to the vehicle's 12-volt automotive system.

The heart of the automotive system is the starter battery. It is designed to provide the brief but heavy surge of electrical power that enables the starter motor to start the engine.

Once the engine is running, the alternator produces electricity that quickly recharges the automotive battery and, at the same time, operates the vehicle's 12-volt equipment.

**The 12-volt coach system** uses a deep-cycle battery to operate the coach's interior lights, water pump, furnace fan and other 12-volt accessories.

When the RV's engine is running, its alternator, in addition to recharging the automotive starting battery, also recharges the coach's deep-cycle battery.

**The RV coach battery**, because it is called upon to deliver a continuous flow of power over extended periods of time and to withstand long periods of deep recharging, should be a 12-volt <u>deep-cycle</u> battery.

The most common type of RV deep-cycle batteries are identified as either Group 24 or Group 27.

The capacity (or rating) of a 12-volt battery is expressed in amp-hours. The bulb in an RV's ceiling light draws about 1 amp of electricity. An 80 amp-hour battery, therefore, should theoretically provide enough energy to illuminate that light bulb for 80 hours.

Most new RVs come equipped with a Group 24 deep-cycle battery. This battery has a rating of about 80 amp-hours. It should be adequate for a weekend of self-contained camping.

A Group 27 deep-cycle battery, however, has a rated capacity of about 105 amp-hours. The Group 27 battery may cost a little more but it has about 30 percent more amp-hour capacity. An RV equipped with two Group 27 deep-cycle batteries will have a capacity of about 210 amp-hours.

Another deep-cycle battery is the 6-volt golf-cart battery. Connecting two of them in series results in 12-volt output and approximately a 220 amp-hour capacity. Some RVs are equipped at the factory with twin golf-cart batteries.

Battery maintenance consists of keeping the electrolyte at the proper level with distilled water and periodically cleaning the battery terminals and cable ends with a solution of baking soda and water.

Be sure all batteries are fully charged before storing your RV. If they are stored in a partially charged condition, they will eventually "sulphate" and lose their ability to accept a full charge.

Disconnecting each battery's ground cable during storage will prevent the batteries from being accidentally discharged by an electrical accessory.

Just follow the RV manufacturer's instructions, maintain your battery and when you turn on the switch it should work.

**An isolator**, located in the engine compartment, prevents the coach's electrical system from stealing the starter battery's power. You wouldn't want to spend a few days camping self contained and then discover you couldn't start your engine.

By the way, in a pinch, you can use your deep-cycle battery to jump start your engine. Some motorhomes even come equipped with a manual or automatic switch that simplifies the procedure.

**The 120-Volt electrical system** acquires its 120-volt electricity from a campground's electrical outlet (electric hookup) or the RV's generator. This is the same type of electricity you obtain from the conventional electric wall outlet in your house.

The RV's roof air-conditioner, microwave oven and other appliances (toaster, hair dryer, etc.) that plug into a conventional household wall outlet will not operate on a coach's 12-volt battery power. They require 120-volt (household electrical) power.

When your RV is connected to a 120-volt electrical source, the RV's electrical wall outlets (like the ones in your house) provide electricity to operate those 120-volt appliances.

At the same time, the RV's **120-volt to 12-volt converter** automatically converts 120-volt AC electricity to 12-volt DC power and feeds it into the coach's 12-volt system. The RV's 12-volt lights and appliances, while still operating on 12-volt electricity, are now drawing their power from the 120-volt source.

Connecting to 120-volt power also activates a **battery charger**, usually integrated with the converter, that automatically recharges the coach's deep-cycle battery. This particular battery charger, by the way, is slow and could take five hours or longer to recharge the coach battery.

**The coach's electrical panel** typically contains the 120-volt breaker switches and the 12-volt fuses. You should learn how to reset a breaker switch and change a fuse, in case the need arises.

**An RV's 120-volt AC generator** is operated by its own gasoline, diesel or propane- fueled engine. It provides 120-volt electricity to the coach's 120-volt electrical system. The amount of electrical power a generator will produce is measured in watts.

The size generator you have should be determined by the amount of watts  your RV appliances require to operate. A single RV roof air conditioner, for example, may require 1,800 to 2,000 watts. It would make sense, then, to have an RV generator capable of producing at least 2,000 watts of electrical power.   If you would also like to operate a 1,200-watt microwave while the 2,000-watt air-conditioner is running, you'll need at least a 3,200-watt generator.

Your generator's instructions will probably recommend running the generator under load (operating a roof air-conditioner, for example) for a couple of hours every month or so.  It is also very important that the generator engine's oil level be checked periodically.

**An Inverter** is a device that converts the coach's 12-volt DC electricity to 120-volt AC electricity.  This allows you to operate 120-volt appliances using power from your coach batteries.

Like a generator, an inverter's output is measured in watts. Small appliances such as televisions, stereos and laptop

computers will operate on inverters rated at 150 to
Frequently this size inverter plugs into a cigarette-ligh
Some RVs come equipped with a built-in inverter, \ ～any to
power a color television. Larger inverters are available for
microwaves, vacuum cleaners and hair dryers.

**Solar Panels** convert sunlight into electrical energy. Panels
vary in size and output. A small panel may simply provide a
trickle charge to keep the RV batteries charged during storage.
A group of larger panels connected to a bank of batteries can
supply most of the electrical needs of a self-contained camper.
Solar panels can be ideal for the RVer who camps for extended
periods of time without hookups.

## Fresh Water System

Where does RV water come from and where does it go?
Easy. It comes out of a faucet and goes down the drain.

The plumbing in an RV is basically the same as that in your
house. The pipes, appliances and fixtures are simply smaller.

Essentially, everything works the same as in your house.
Turn on a faucet and you have water, hot or cold, depending
upon the faucet you choose. And, just like at home, the sink or
shower empties down the drain.

There are some differences, however, and a basic
understanding of how your RV's fresh-water and waste-water
systems work can make RVing easier for you.

Here is a non-technical description of an RV's plumbing
system, a simple explanation of how it works and what you can
do to keep things flowing smoothly.

There are two water sources for an RV, the onboard fresh-
water tank and the outside water hookup. Let's take a look at
them.

**The onboard fresh-water tank** carries water for the RV's faucets, water heater and toilet. Water is added to the tank through a filler spout on the exterior of the RV.

Your RV may be equipped with a valve that permits you to fill the water tank while the RV is connected to the campground's water hookup. Before opening this valve, be sure to remove the cap on the exterior water-tank filler spout opening. This will allow air to escape from the tank as it fills with water. The water tank could expand like a balloon and damage the RV if air isn't allowed to escape.

Since organisms, especially in warm weather, have a tendency to thrive in standing water, it is generally recommended that you drain your water tanks before the RV is stored for any length of time..

**A 12-volt water pump** is usually located at the base of the water tank. Turning on an electrical switch in the RV enables the coach's deep-cycle battery to provide 12-volt electricity to the water pump.

When the switch is on, the pump automatically activates whenever a faucet is opened. It pumps water from the water tank and through the RV's plumbing system. The pump will continue to operate until you turn off the faucet.

To avoid water leak damage, turn the water pump's electric switch off while traveling and when the RV is in storage. Some RVers, just to be on the safe side, turn the switch off whenever they leave their RV.

**When outside water hookups are available** at a campground or RV park, a drinking-water hose is connected between the campground's water faucet (hookup) and the RV's water inlet. The hose delivers the campground's water (and water pressure) into the same RV plumbing system as the RV's water pump. A one-way valve prevents the water from pushing past the water pump and into the water tank.

When you are connected to an outside water hookup, turn on a faucet in your RV and you have water.

**The drinking-water hose** resembles a garden hose and costs about the same. It is usually white and will come in a package that identifies it as a drinking-water hose. Drinking-water hoses are constructed of materials that will not impart any taste to the water.

When you store the water hose, connect both ends together. This will prevent any remaining moisture from dripping into the compartment and it will keep insects and dirt out of the hose.

**A water-pressure regulator** is an inexpensive investment in protecting your RV's plumbing. If you install the water-pressure regulator on the campground end of the water hose, it will protect both the hose and the RV's plumbing from any surges in the campground's water pressure.

**Water filters** offer a variety of technologies. They are connected between the RV water-hose and the campground's water hookup. The simplest and least expensive will filter out sediment and bad tastes but not micro-organisms. The most expensive can cost hundreds of dollars and may even use ultraviolet light to kill harmful micro-organisms.

Water quality varies throughout the North American continent. It certainly doesn't appear to be improving. Whether to use a water filter and what type is a personal judgment call.

Many RVers don't use any filter at all and seem to do well. Some will purchase bottled water for consumption and use water from their faucets strictly for washing.

**RV water heaters** usually hold six or ten gallons of water and use propane to heat the water. Today's water heaters are ignited by an on/off switch in the RV. When the water is hot, the flame will automatically turn off. The flame automatically cycles on and off, keeping the water hot, until the switch is turned off.

You can conserve propane by switching the water heater on about an hour before hot water is needed and switching the water heater off during the remainder of the day.

Some RV water heaters are also equipped with an electrical heating element. This can be a real propane saver when you have an electrical hookup. These heating elements can be added to your existing propane water heater. They are available from RV accessory and parts suppliers.

**Water heater maintenance** - Drain and flush the water heater once a year or so. Turn off the water supply (water hookup or water pump). Open the water heater's pressure relief valve and the drain valve. When the water has stopped draining, turn on the water supply (water hookup or water pump) with the drain valve still open. Let the water flow through the water heater for a few minutes to flush out any corrosive particles.

Turn off the water, close the pressure relief and drain valves. When you turn on the water supply, it will refill the water tank.

**RV water faucets** operate just like the ones in your house. RV shower heads are equipped with a shutoff valve that enables you to conserve water and the propane used to heat the shower water. Turn on a faucet and you have water.

**The RV toilet** is usually a marine type toilet with two pedals at its base. Pressing one pedal adds water to the toilet bowl; pressing the other pedal opens a valve in the bottom of the toilet and empties the bowl directly into the black-water holding tank. Try to keep about an inch of water in the bottom of the toilet bowl. It will keep the seal moist and prevent unwanted odors from entering the RV.

Don't put anything into the toilet except pre-digested food, toilet paper and liquids.

**Sanitizing the water system** should be done when you purchase a used RV, after long periods of not using the water tank and whenever you suspect something may have contaminated the water system.

Start by completely draining the water tank. Then, for every 15 gallons of water-tank capacity, pour one-quarter cup of liquid household chlorine bleach into a gallon container. Fill the container with water and stir.

Pour the bleach and water mixture into the RV's empty water tank. Fill the water tank with clean fresh water. Drive the rig through the neighborhood to slosh the mixture throughout the tank.

Using the water pump, open each faucet for 30 seconds to get the bleach into the water pipes. Run the hot water faucets long enough to replace the water heater's six or ten gallons of water with the chlorine mix from the water tank.

Top off the water tank with fresh water. Let the mixture sit for at least three hours.

Drain the entire water system, including the hot-water tank. Fill the water tank with clean, fresh water and pump it through the water heater and faucets. Let the clean water stand for a couple of hours. Drain and refill with fresh water.

## Waste-Water System

The waste-water system on an RV gives you the option of hooking up to a campground's sewer system or storing your waste water in the RV's holding tanks until it can be dumped at a disposal facility.

Most RVs are equipped with two waste-water holding tanks; the gray-water tank and the black-water tank.

**The gray-water holding tank** collects waste water from the sink(s) and shower.

**The black-water holding tank** collects waste from the toilet. (The bathroom sink on some RVs may also drain into the black-water tank.)

**Dumping valves** are provided on the exterior of the RV for each holding tank. (Some RVs may have the valves located inside a heated exterior cabinet.) When the valves are closed (pushed in) the tanks will collect and hold waste water until a waste-water disposal station or a campground's sewer hookup is available. Pulling out the valve handle allows the contents of the tank to empty (dump) through the RV's sewer outlet.

**A sewer hose** is used to connect the RV's sewer outlet to a campground's sewer inlet (sewer hookup) or to a waste-water disposal station's sewer inlet. The sewer hose material comes in different thicknesses. The thicker or heavier material is generally more resistant to punctures and tears.

Both holding tanks' valves <u>should remain closed</u> except when dumping. Leaving the valves open could result in a buildup of solid waste in the bottom of the tanks. Sediment could also collect in the grooves of the tank valves and prevent them from closing.

You'll find that many RVers, however, prefer to leave the dumping valve on their <u>gray-water</u> holding tank open while their RV is connected to a campground's sewer hookup. This allows the water from the sinks and shower to drain immediately into the campground's sewer.

Waiting to empty the black-water tank until it is half to three-quarters full will provide a more complete flushing action.

Whenever possible, empty both holding tanks before traveling. There's no sense in hauling unnecessary weight.

After emptying the holding tanks, add a few gallons of water to each of them to keep the seals moist and to prevent any remaining waste from solidifying on the bottom of the tank.

Use holding tank deodorants and additives approved for RV holding tanks. They are available at RV accessory stores.

**Holding tank maintenance** - Both holding tanks and the sewer hose should be washed and rinsed once in a while, especially before a long period of storage.

Fill the tanks two-thirds full with soapy water. Drive through the neighborhood to slosh the water in the tanks. Empty the tanks (at a disposal station).

Refill the tanks to two-thirds full with plain water, slosh and dump again. Add a few gallons of plain water to each holding tank.

## Propane System

Propane appliances are major contributors to the comfort and convenience of RVing. Turn a knob, ignite a burner and you can cook dinner. Press a button, ignite the water heater and you can take a hot shower. Turn a selector knob, set a dial and your refrigerator makes ice. Flip a switch, set the thermostat and your home on wheels is warm and cozy. All this is made possible by that magical gas we call propane.

Here is a non-technical description of your RV's propane system, a simple description of how it works and some tips on how to maintain it. We've also included the same type of information about your RV's propane-operated refrigerator.

**Propane** (also known as Liquified Petroleum Gas or LPG) costs a little more than gasoline and lasts a very long time. One-half gallon a day would be fairly heavy consumption in summertime and about average during the colder months.

You'll find propane is readily available whenever you need it. Look for it at campgrounds, RV dealerships, RV accessory stores and even gas stations across the nation.

**The RV's propane tank(s)** hold the propane in a liquid state under pressure. Opening the faucet-like valve on the tank allows the propane to flow, as a gas, through pipes to the appliances. There are two types of propane containers. One is the DOT container called a cylinder. Vertical DOT cylinders are typically found on trailers. The other container is the ASME container called a tank. Horizontal ASME tanks are generally found on motorhomes.

The propane cylinders on a trailer may be removed and conveniently transported to a propane filling station. It is important, though, that the cylinders remain in the same upright position as on the trailer.

The propane tank on a motorhome is permanently attached to the vehicle. You'll have to drive your motorhome to the propane filling station when it's time to refill.

**During propane filling** the attendant should open the propane tank's liquid-level or 20% valve. When the tank is 80% full, you'll see propane begin to escape through the 20% valve as a white liquid. The filling process should be stopped at this point. The liquid-level valve shouldn't be closed until the escaping liquid becomes a vapor. The maximum amount of propane a tank should hold is 80% of its capacity.

Since propane is sold either by the pound or the gallon, the numbers stamped into the protective collar of the propane tank can be useful.

Begin by looking for the date of manufacture. DOT propane cylinders (but not ASME tanks) must be inspected and stamped 12 years after manufacture and every 5 years thereafter. (Used RV buyers take note.)

The numbers to the right of "WC" (Water Capacity) indicate the amount of water, in pounds, the tank is capable of containing.

A tank with WC 47.7 stamped on it has a water capacity of 47.7 pounds of water. By dividing the water capacity by 8.3 (the weight of one gallon of water) you can determine how many gallons the tank is capable of holding. (47.7 divided by 8.3 equals 5.74 gallons of liquid.)

A propane tank or cylinder, however, may only be filled to 80% of its capacity with propane. So multiply the number of gallons the tank is capable of holding by 80% to determine how many gallons of propane the tank may hold. (5.74 gallons of capacity times 80% equals 4.59 gallons of propane.)

Multiply that number by 4.24 (the weight of one gallon of propane) to determine the tank's propane weight capacity (4.59 gallons times 4.24 equals 19.46 pounds of propane).

The numbers to the right of "TW" (Tare Weight) indicate the weight of the empty tank. Adding the weight of the empty tank to its propane weight capacity tells you how much the properly filled tank would weigh (18 pounds "TW" plus 19.46 pounds of propane capacity equals 37.46 pounds for a full tank).

You can determine approximately how many gallons of propane remain in a cylinder by weighing it on a bathroom scale. Subtract the Tare Weight (weight of the empty cylinder) and divide the remainder by 4.24 (weight of one gallon of propane).

**The gas appliances** in your RV perform the same functions as your home appliances. Their operation will also be similar. It is important, however, that you read your instructions and/or ask your dealer to show you the correct operating procedure for the gas appliances in your RV.

The forced-air furnace and the hot-water heater are the largest consumers of propane. One way you can conserve propane is to use an electric space heater. Another is to turn on the water heater 45 minutes to an hour before you need hot water and then turn it off when you're done. This prevents the water heater from cycling on and off all day and night.

**A propane gas-leak detector** (if the RV has one) will set off an alarm and automatically shut off the propane near the tank if it detects propane. Since propane is heavier than air, the detector is located near the floor in the living area of the RV. Eventually, propane becomes lighter than air and rises to nose level. Propane smells like rotten onions or garlic. If you suspect a propane leak, vacate the RV, turn off the propane at the tank and leave the RV door open to allow the gas to escape. A qualified service person should be used to locate and repair any suspected propane problems.

Turn off the propane at the tank before driving down the road. This will minimize the dangers of propane leaks that may be caused by vibration or a collision. If you insist on driving with the propane on, be sure to extinguish any flames before entering a gas station.

**Propane system maintenance** - Periodically check for leaks by turning the propane on at the tank and brushing a soapy water solution on the pipe joints. The appearance of bubbles indicates a leak. Have a qualified RV technician check and repair the propane system.

Whenever possible, store the RV with the propane tanks full. This will minimize the formation of condensation inside the tank(s).

## RV Refrigerator

Believe it or not, the RV refrigerator uses heat to make ice cubes.

The RV's absorption-type refrigerator operates when a heat source causes a mixture of hydrogen gas, liquid ammonia and water to circulate through a closed loop of tubing in the refrigerator.

The heat source can be either a propane flame, a 12-volt heating element or a 120-volt heating element. Check the operating instructions of your refrigerator. The heat source(s) will be identified and their method(s) of operation described.

The gas/liquid mixture circulates from the outside rear wall of the refrigerator, through the freezer compartment and back to the outside rear wall of the refrigerator. This circulating mixture absorbs heat from the freezer and releases it into the air outside the refrigerator's rear wall. The removal of this heat allows the refrigerator to get cold enough to make ice cubes.

Operating the refrigerator when it is not level can interfere with the circulation of the gas/fluid mixture. The result can range from inefficient cooling to permanent refrigerator damage. To assure the long life of your refrigerator, be sure it is level while operating.

Operating the refrigerator while driving down the road will not harm it. The rocking action of the coach will keep the gas/fluid mixture circulating.

Most RV refrigerators offer the choice of operating on either a propane flame or a 120-volt electrical heating element. Some offer a third heat source, a 12-volt heating element.

Your refrigerator will have a selector switch so you can choose the heat source.

Some RVers operate their refrigerators with 120-volt power when they have electrical hookups, the propane flame when electrical hookups are not available and 12-volt power while driving down the road.

Keep in mind that the 12-volt heating element draws so much electricity it can completely discharge a battery in one day. The only practical time to operate the refrigerator on 12-

volt power is when the engine is running and the alternator is recharging the battery.

Since the refrigerator does not burn a noticeable amount of propane, many RVers find it convenient to simply run their refrigerator on propane all the time.

**Safety conscious RVers** turn off the gas appliances and shut the propane off at the tank before driving down the road. The contents of the refrigerator will remain cold and the freezer items will stay frozen for many hours with the refrigerator turned off. If you do insist on traveling with the refrigerator's propane burner lit, at least have the common sense to extinguish the flame before going into a gas station. The open flame could ignite the gasoline fumes.

Here are a few thoughts that will help you get the most out of your refrigerator:

- The refrigerator works best when level.
- Leave space for the cold air to circulate in the food compartment.
- During hot weather, shade the refrigerator side of the RV
- You may have to periodically adjust the refrigerator's temperature setting when days are warm and nights are cold.
- Secure the refrigerator door before driving down the road.
- Turn off the refrigerator, clean the food compartment and prop open the door to prevent mold when the RV is in storage.

The propane system is easy to use. Propane is relatively inexpensive, lasts a long time and burns clean. Turn it on at the tank and ignite your appliances. Before you go on the road or store your RV, turn off the appliances and turn off the propane at the tank. It's that easy!

# Chapter 4

# DRIVING YOUR RV

Driving an RV is different than driving an automobile. Different but not difficult. It's different because the RV is higher, wider, longer and heavier. It's not difficult because the vehicle's controls, the driving techniques and the rules of the road are similar to those of an automobile. Anyone who can drive a car should easily adapt to driving an RV.

It takes practice in a variety of circumstances to become a proficient RV driver. Novice RV owners, obviously, will benefit from any time spent learning how to drive their new rig. Experienced RVers should also take the time to become familiar with the unique handling characteristics and driving capabilities of each new RV they acquire.

Before driving your new RV, adjust the driver's seat and mirrors. Ask someone to walk around the perimeter of your rig while you sit in the driver's seat. Follow them in your mirrors so you can locate your "blind" spots.

Next, check the air pressure in all of your tires. Incorrect or uneven tire pressure can adversely affect the way your RV handles and brakes.

Finally, measure the distance from the ground to the top of the highest solid object on the RV's roof. If there's a flexible antenna that extends even higher, note that distance too.

Record the measurements on a 3x5 card. Keep the measurement card handy, perhaps on the sun visor, for quick reference when a road sign suddenly warns of a low bridge or narrow tunnel ahead.

## Parking Lot Practice

Locate an empty parking lot to practice turning and backing your rig. Use traffic cones, cardboard boxes or empty plastic jugs to create mockups of curbs, corners and campsites in the parking lot.

An RV, because it is longer than an automobile, will require wider turns to avoid having the rear tires cut across the inside corner.

When making right turns, begin by keeping a little farther to the left of the curb than you would with a car. Drive a little farther into the intersection before turning the steering wheel to the right.

Begin left turns from the usual position in the left turn lane but drive a little farther into the intersection before turning the steering wheel to the left.

Use your mirrors to check your side clearance as you make your turns. Notice how the rear end of the RV swings out in the opposite direction of the turn. This is important to keep in mind when maneuvering in tight areas. Practice these turns in the parking lot.

Use the parking lot to drive in tight right-hand and left-hand circles. This will reveal your RV's turning radius.

As you gain confidence, move to the busier streets and highways.

## Backing An RV

Backing an RV gets easier with experience. Practice in the parking lot with the help of an observer. The observer should be in a position to spot obstacles (and little kids) the driver can't see.

There are a number of successful backing procedures utilizing an observer. This one is simple and it works:

The observer takes up a position slightly to the rear of the RV and on the driver's side. The driver should be able to see the observer in the driver's side-view mirror. The observer maintains this position, remaining in visual contact with the driver, as the RV is backing. The observer simply has to point in the direction the rear of the RV should move.

Some RVers use a hand-held CB radio for the observer to communicate with the driver while backing.

Backing into a campsite is easier if you back to the left. Backing to the left allows the driver to observe the left rear corner of the rig and where it is headed.

Back slowly. When in doubt, stop, get out and look. Don't be afraid to pull forward to correct any errors. There's no rule about backing an RV that says you can't pull forward occasionally.

To back a trailer, place your hands at the bottom of the steering wheel. To move the rear of the trailer to the left; move the bottom of the steering wheel to the left. To move the rear of the trailer to the right; move the bottom of the steering wheel to the right. Try it. It works!

Build confidence in your backing skills by backing through a figure-eight course in the parking lot.

Practice driving on quiet side streets after the parking lot session. Be aware of your height and width clearances. Look for overhanging branches and street signs. You wouldn't think twice about them in a car, but in an RV, they can drag across your rooftop air conditioners or redecorate the side of your rig.

Make plenty of left and right turns. Seek out the location of your "blind spots." Test your brakes. Practice backing into your driveway as though it were a campsite.

You'll soon learn that maneuvering an RV, while a little different than an automobile, is not difficult.

## Highway Driving

Take your RV out on the highway.

Use the highway on-ramp to steadily accelerate so you can enter the highway at the speed of the traffic. Use your side-view mirror to pick your "slot" and gradually merge into traffic.

On the highway, settle into one lane and stay with the flow of traffic. Generally speaking, the law requires vehicles towing a trailer (including motorhomes pulling a car) to stay in the far right lane except when passing. The exception to this may be when there are four or more lanes in one direction. Then you may drive in either of the two lanes closest to the right side of the road.

On multi-lane highways, the lane just to the left of the slow lane is generally the most comfortable for RVers. This eliminates having to adjust your speed to accommodate traffic entering and exiting the highway.

You can center your RV in a lane by using your side-view mirrors. The mirrors will show you the relationship of the sides of the RV to the white lines on the highway.

Get into the habit of frequently checking your mirrors and being aware of traffic conditions on either side and to your rear. Big-rig drivers check their side-view mirrors as often as every 30 seconds.

See and be seen. Driving with your headlights on during daytime is an effective safety precaution. Always signal lane changes and turns.

Allow more room to stop your heavy rig and more time for your longer RV to pass other vehicles.

Use lower gears for engine power to climb hills and for braking power when descending.

Going uphill, downshift before the engine begins to lug. Move to the far right lane. Don't let traffic stack up behind you.

It's dangerous for everyone, including you. Pull over and let the other vehicles pass.

Going downhill, keep your rig at a safe, manageable speed. Downshift early to prevent speed from building up too quickly. Generally speaking, the gear you select to go up one side of a hill is the one you should use when descending the other side.

Avoid riding the brake pedal. This could cause overheating and brake fade. Apply the brakes firmly enough to drop your speed five to ten miles per hour. Then take your foot off the brake pedal and allow a slow buildup of speed before applying the brakes again.

If your RV is equipped with air brakes, the braking procedure is slightly different. Rather than frequently pumping the brake pedal, which could deplete the compressed air supply, apply the brakes for longer periods before releasing them. Air brakes are more capable of handling high temperatures and dispersing heat.

Decelerate on a straightaway before entering a curve. Braking while under the influence of centrifugal force, especially while going downhill, can cause stability problems. Ideally, you should have slowed to the appropriate speed just as you enter the curve.

Stay alert for windy conditions. Be prepared for sudden gusts of wind when you cross bridges, exit tunnels and when big trucks pass you at high speed.

Trailerists can counteract side-to-side sway by using the hand control to simultaneously activate their trailer brakes (independent of the tow vehicle's brakes) while accelerating slightly.

Notice how and where the truck and bus drivers drive. There's a lot to be learned by observing those who drive for a living.

Be patient in heavy traffic. Eventually all those folks will be at work and you'll be on the open road.

Driving an RV is an acquired skill. It is different than driving an automobile. Different but not difficult.

# Chapter 5

# EQUIPPING YOUR RV

You can tell who the serious RVers are by the amount of stuff they carry in their outside storage compartments. There'll be basic stuff, backup stuff, extra stuff and tools to help put the stuff together. Serious RVers refer to their stuff as essential RV equipment.

When you buy an RV, new or used, it will usually come with a water hose, sewer hose and a few connectors. This is basic equipment. It won't be long before you'll want to go out and buy a lot more stuff.

Here is a list to get you started. We've put an asterisk (*) next to those articles we feel are the minimum needed to do the job. You should find most of the items at RV accessory stores or at hardware, plumbing and electrical stores.

## Hookup and Leveling Equipment

### Electrical Hookup Equipment

*25-foot, 30-amp, 12-gauge electrical cord. This is standard, built-in equipment for most RVs. One end is usually hard-wired to the RV. The other end plugs into the campground's electrical outlet.

*30-amp-plug to 20-amp-receptacle adapter. Some campgrounds do not have 30-amp outlets but do have 20-amp outlets. This adapter permits your RV's 30-amp cord to be plugged into a 20-amp electrical outlet.

**Spare 25-foot, 30-amp, 12-gauge extension cord.** There may be occasions when one 25-foot electrical cord is not long enough.

**Polarity tester** - Before plugging in your RV's electrical cord, use the polarity tester to determine if the campground's electrical outlet is wired properly. An improperly-wired outlet can result in a shocking and sometimes deadly experience.

**Voltage meter** - (The type that can be plugged into a standard wall outlet.) Some campgrounds, especially older ones, may be equipped with 120-volt, 30-amp outlets but, on occasion, will not deliver sufficient voltage for the RV's appliances. The roof air conditioner, for example, needs a minimum of 105 volts or the compressor could burn out. It is a good idea to periodically check the available voltage, especially during hot weather when everyone in the campground is using their air-conditioners,.

**15 to 20 feet of TV antenna hookup cable.** Many RV parks offer a cable TV antenna connection. You wouldn't want to miss anything.

## Fresh-Water Hookup Equipment

**\*25-foot drinking-water hose.** For connecting the RV to the campground's water hookup and for filling the fresh-water tank. If you've purchased a used RV, buy a new drinking-water hose. You don't know what has been living (or dying) in the old hose. Get a hose that is labeled "Drinking-Water Hose". It shouldn't cost much more than a standard garden hose and it won't impart any tastes to your water.

**Spare 25-foot drinking water hose.** There may be occasions when one 25-foot hose is not long enough.

*Tip: Cut a 25-foot length of water hose into 10 and 15-foot lengths. Install hose-repair connectors (available at most hardware stores) on the cut ends to create a 10-foot and a 15-*

*foot length of water hose. This will give you the option of a 10, 15 or (by joining the two together) a 25-foot water-hose connection.*

**\*Water-pressure regulator.** Occasionally, a campground's water system will experience a sudden surge in water pressure. A water-pressure regulator is inexpensive insurance against damaged RV plumbing.

**Water filter.** A personal judgment call. Inexpensive water filters will filter out particles and bad tastes but not harmful micro-organisms. Many RVers have a water filter of some kind but not all RVers use them.

**'Y' connector with shutoffs.** Allows two hoses to be attached to one campground water hookup.

**Water-hose quick-connects.** Attach these to the ends of your water hose, water filter and water-pressure regulator. They enable quick, easy and water-tight connections.

## Waste-Water Hookup Equipment

**\* 20-foot length of sewer hose** Sewer hoses are made of various thicknesses of vinyl material. The heavier material is more expensive but is more resistant to penetration by sharp stones or thorns.

**Spare 20-foot length of sewer hose.** Just in case.

**\*Sewer-hose connectors.** Install a male sewer-hose connector on one end of each hose and a female sewer-hose connector on the other end. This will permit a quick hookup to the campground and easy connection of additional lengths of hose.

*Tip: When installing the sewer-hose connectors to the ends of the sewer hose, first dip the end of the hose in hot water for a few moments. This will soften the hose and make it easy to slip in the connector. Don't forget to put the retainer ring on the hose before inserting the connector.*

**\*Sewer-inlet adapter.** RV park sewer hookups come with a variety of inlet sizes. Look for an adapter that will fit several sizes of sewer openings. A sewer adapter with a 90-degree shape will allow the sewer hose to lay flat on the ground.

*Tip: Purchase two lengths of sewer hose, one 10-feet long and one 20-feet long. Create a third hose by cutting a three-foot section from one end of the 20-foot hose.*

*Install a female sewer-hose connector on one end of the three hoses and a male sewer-hose connector on the other end of the 10-foot and (now) 17-foot hoses.*

*Install the sewer-inlet adapter at the unoccupied end of the 3-foot hose.*

*Now when you connect to a campground's sewer hookup, you have the option of using a 10-foot, 17-foot or (by joining them together) a 27- foot length of sewer hose. The short length of sewer hose with the sewer-inlet adapter will connect to any of your sewer hose combinations.*

**Sewer-outlet terminator cap (with water-hose connector).** Protects the end of the RV's sewer outlet. The water-hose connector provides the option of draining the gray-water tank through a water hose (don't use that hose for drinking water afterwards). If your RV permits you to leave the sewer hose connected to the RV's sewer outlet, place the terminator cap on the open end of the sewer hose between uses.

**Disposable gloves** to wear when handling sewer hoses.

## Leveling Equipment

**\*Bubble levels**, permanently mounted on your rig, will make leveling easier. You'll want two levels, one for side-to-side leveling and the other for front-to-rear. Begin by getting the RV (and refrigerator) as level as possible. Now install the levels with their indicators reading dead center.

Trailer owners can install one level on the exterior of the trailer's front wall to help with side-to-side leveling. Another can be mounted on the exterior of the trailer's side wall where it can be monitored while leveling front-to-rear.

Motorhome owners can mount the side-to-side level on the dash and install the front-to-rear level on the interior wall to the driver's left. This will assist the driver in maneuvering the motorhome into the most level position.

*Leveling boards.** Leveling an RV can be as easy as driving the lower wheel(s) up onto a couple of boards. You'll develop your own RV lumber pile but here's a starting suggestion:

Motorhome or single axle trailer:

One 2x6 board, 11 inches long

One 2x6 board, 22 inches long

One 2x6 board, 33 inches long

Nail the three boards together to create a leveling ramp with three 11 inch long steps. Build two ramps for a motorhome.

Trailer (tandem axles):

One 2x6 board, 40 inches long (or long enough for both tires to fit on it)

Four 2x6 boards, 24 inches long

One 2x6 board, 8 inches long

Do not nail these boards together. You'll have sufficient boards to create a variety of ramps up to 5 inches high.

**Plywood Boards**, 3/4 inch thick and approximately eight inches to a foot square will provide a solid foundation under leveling, stabilizing or trailer tongue jacks when you're parked on soft ground or blacktop.

*Wheel Chocks (at least two) to block the wheels. Trailers don't have parking brakes. Wedging these in front of and back of the tires should prevent the RV from rolling away. Wheel chocks can be created by cutting a 45-degree angle at the end of a one-foot long , 4" x 4" piece of lumber.

Trailer-Hitch Lock to prevent someone from hooking up to and driving off with your trailer or fifth-wheel.

## Tools and Spare Parts

### Tools

*Tire pressure gauge. Be sure it will record the high pressures of your tires.

*Standard tire-changing tools (for both vehicles).

*Basic mechanical tools (wrenches, pliers, screwdrivers, etc.). Even if you're not mechanically inclined, you'll want to have something available when a good samaritan comes along.

*Jumper cables

*Flares or warning reflectors

*Flashlight and extra batteries

*Duct tape

Small air compressor

Trenching tool or small shovel

Small saw

Hatchet

Water bucket

### Spare Parts

Auto parts stores are found everywhere. Obtaining spare parts shouldn't be a problem in the populated areas of the

United States and Canada. Just in case your size may be difficult to obtain, you may want to carry:

**Engine belts and hoses.**

**Fuel filter.**

**Wheel bearings for trailers.**

## Patio Furniture

**Outside door mat** - Something to knock the dust, dirt and sand from your feet before entering the RV. You may also want to carry a large piece of astroturf or indoor-outdoor carpeting. Select a size anywhere from 3' x 4' to 8' x 12' depending upon your needs and storage capacity.

**Folding lawn chairs** - Don't leave home without them.

**Small folding table** - Handy when set up between a couple of lawn chairs.

**Portable barbecue** - The propane type is cleaner and easier. Adapters are available to connect to a small refillable propane tank, rather than using disposable propane canisters.

Load all of this stuff into your RV's outside storage compartments and you'll look like a serious RVer too.

## Miscellaneous Accessories

Here are some optional accessories we would definitely include in our next RV. You'll notice that none of them are necessities ... unless you happen to be hung up on personal comfort.

**Roof-Vent Covers** - Opening a roof vent allows heat, condensation and tobacco smoke to escape the confines of an RV. Opening a roof vent when it's raining, however, results in a wet floor. Adding a roof-vent cover permits you to open the roof vent when it's raining, windy and even while you're driving down the road.

**12-Volt Fan** - A 12-volt, oscillating fan that can be plugged into a cigarette lighter outlet will move air whether you have hookups or not. We move our small table model from dashboard to kitchen to bedroom depending upon our needs.

**Awnings** - During warm weather we try to choose a campsite so the street-side wall of the coach faces east or north and remains shaded during the warm part of the day. That way, when we roll out our patio awning, the walls on both sides are shaded.

In all of our RVs the refrigerator has been located on the curb-side wall of the coach. On hot days we stretch out the patio awning not only to protect the entry-door wall from the heat of the sun but to help the refrigerator to continue functioning efficiently.

Our next RV will also have awnings to shade as many of the windows as possible. Glass can radiate an amazing amount of heat into an RV.

**Windshield Covers** - There are interior and exterior windshield covers available. Some shade the inside of the RV yet allow you to see through them to the outside. Others are heavy gauge vinyl that you can't see through.

We have both types and use them according to our needs. We selected the ones that mount on the inside of the windshield so we wouldn't have to be concerned about them getting dirty or wet. The heavy vinyl windshield cover, in conjunction with the windshield drapes, creates a fairly effective barrier against the cold.

**Portable Electric Heater** - Once your RV's propane-fired heater has warmed up the interior of your RV, a small electric heater will keep things cozy for a long time. Since the RV's forced air furnace is one of the heaviest consumers of propane, you'll appreciate the added benefit of not having to refill your tanks too often.

**120-Volt, AC Water-Heater Element** - The RV's water heater is another heavy consumer of propane. It burns propane for a half hour or longer to heat the initial tank of water. The flame then periodically roars to life throughout the day and night to maintain the water's temperature setting.

A 120-volt, AC heating element, added to the RV's existing water heater, saves propane and silently maintains the water temperature whenever you have an electrical hookup.

**CB Radio** - Eavesdrop on the conversation of truckers, ascertain road conditions from oncoming traffic or chit-chat with fellow travelers. These are just a few of the many uses for CB radios. In addition to the CB installed in our driving compartment, we have a hand-held unit. Vicki frequently stands at the rear of our RV and uses the hand-held unit to communicate with me when we are backing into a tight campsite.

**Cellular Telephone** - A cellular telephone allows you to place or receive emergency telephone calls almost everywhere in the USA. This translates into peace of mind for RV travelers who are concerned about children or parents.

Placing or receiving cellular phone calls can be very expensive while on the road. We rely on pay phones for everyday calls and reserve the cellular phone for emergencies only. (When it's wet and cold outside and we need to make a call, we have been known to consider that an emergency.)

You really don't need any of this stuff to enjoy RVing. We didn't have any of it when we bought our first or even our second RV. Somehow, as you go down the road, accessories and gadgets accumulate and the next thing you know ... they become necessities.

## Domestic Furnishings and Supplies

The living area of the RV should be outfitted, or furnished, with the intention of leaving the items in the rig permanently, just as you would in a vacation home. The objective should be to have everything you need already on board and ready to go. When it's time to go on a trip, all you need to add are a few personal toiletries, some clothes and food.

There are a number of approaches to outfitting or furnishing the living area of the RV. Everything can be purchased brand new. Items for the RV can be taken from the house and replaced with brand new items. You can haunt garage sales and thrift shops. Any combination of the above.

The following list may not be complete, but it is a great start:

Blankets
Sheets (fitted are easiest)
Sleeping Bags

Bath towels
Hand towels
Wash cloths
Dish cloths
Pot holders

Wooden matches
Paper towels
Paper napkins
Aluminum foil
Zippered plastic food bags
Plastic wastebasket liners
Large trash bags
Toilet Paper
Facial tissues

Dishes (plates, cups, bowls, etc.)
Paper plates (cups, bowls, etc.)
Drinking glasses (glass, plastic)
Coffee mugs
Dessert/Cereal bowls
Silverware
Steak knives
Refrigerator containers and lids
Pitcher and lid

Cooking Utensils
    Can opener
    Spatula
    Tongs
        Kitchen knives
    Cooking fork
    Cooking spoons
    Measuring cups
    Measuring spoons

Pans (Teflon)
Skillets (Teflon)
Cookie sheet (Teflon)
Square cake pan (Teflon)
Stovetop coffee pot
Electric coffee pot
Toaster
Teakettle

Cleaning supplies:
    Dishpan(s)
    Dish drainer & mat
    Dish soap
    Cleanser
    Scouring pads

    Window cleaner
    Broom
    Dustpan
    Vacuum cleaner

Laundry supplies:
    Laundry soap
    Fabric softener
    Bleach

Iron and tabletop ironing board

Personal toiletries:
    Soap
    Shampoo
    Toothbrushes
    Toothpaste
    Deodorant
    Hair dryer
    Curling iron
    Hair brushes
    Combs
    Rechargeable shaver

Prescription medications
Over-the-counter medicine

First aid kit
Insect repellent

Office items:
    Paper
    Pens
    Pencils
    Envelopes
    Postage stamps
    Stapler
    Ruler
    Paper clips

*Tip:    Maintain an ongoing list in the RV of items that need to be replaced. Those that aren't replaced during the trip can be purchased at home and put in the RV before the next trip.*

## Packing An RV

We all want to take as much stuff as possible when we go on the road. But an RV, no matter how big, has a limited amount of closets, cupboards and drawers. Even with creative packing, there's a limit to how much it can hold.

And ... there's a limit to how much weight, including passengers, you can add to the RV. That limit is called cargo capacity.

So, before you start packing, find out how much weight you can load into your rig.

Refer to the chapter on Vehicle Weights and Ratings to determine your RV's cargo capacity.

Once you know how much weight you can add to the RV, the fun part can begin.

One of the secrets of successful RV packing is minimizing the things you have to pack.

Before you pack an item, ask yourself... is it absolutely necessary? Can I do without it? How often will I use it? Will some other item do the job? Will this item do double duty?

While you're packing, try to keep the RV's center of gravity low by storing heavy items at or below floor level.

The contents of an RV's cabinets and cupboards have a tendency to rearrange themselves as you drive down the road. Pack everything to minimize movement. Non-skid material placed on the cupboard shelves works well. It's available at RV accessory stores.

Partitions made of cardboard, masonite or wood will keep things stationary and increase storage space.

Pack things in containers -- boxes, bins or bags.

Transparent plastic storage boxes come in various sizes, are lightweight, durable and interchangeable.They can be packed in your house and carried to the RV for the trip. Kept in overhead cabinets, you can see what's inside and pull them out like a drawer.  At the end of the trip, they can be carried into your house and unpacked.

Cardboard boxes are lightweight, inexpensive and can be cut to fit if necessary. Covering them with self-sticking vinyl shelf paper reinforces them and makes them more attractive.

Zippered plastic bags and small plastic food containers make efficient use of refrigerator and cupboard space. They also keep out critters and humidity.

Try to create additional space. Buy or build shelves. Plastic-coated wire shelves are available in many RV accessory stores.

You might be able to add shelves, drawers or cabinets to the bottom of the wardrobe closet if you don't need the full-length space.

Hooks for jackets and bathrobes can be placed in corners or out-of-the-way spots.

Pack things according to their priority. Pack the absolute necessities first.  Then the things you think you need and so on.

Pack similar items in the same cupboards, drawers or sections of the RV.

The busiest area of your RV will probably be the kitchen. Begin there.

Put cooking and eating utensils where they make the most sense for convenient preparation and serving of meals.

Next comes food items.  Put them where they are readily accessible.

Dishwashing and kitchen cleaning materials should also be easy to reach.

The bathroom is easy.  You'll want everyday toiletries handy.  If each person keeps their personal toiletries in a separate plastic box, it will make things that much easier.

Daily medicines should be up front or at eye level. Seldom used medications can be relegated to the harder-to-reach locations.

Identify a shelf or cupboard to store extra towels and linens. You don't need to carry more than seven to ten days worth. You'll probably do laundry that often.

In the bedroom, you may be able to get by with no more than seven to ten days worth of clothing. Once again, plan on doing laundry.

Try to take only the clothes you'll need for that trip. Utilize mix-and-match outfits to minimize the number of clothes you need.

You can save hanging-locker space by taking wrinkle-resistant, foldable clothes and putting them in cupboards or drawers.

Begin exterior packing at the utility-hookup cabinet. Leveling and hooking up the RV may take place daily. You'll want the hookup and leveling equipment to be as accessible and convenient as possible.

Leveling boards will get wet and dirty. Create a moisture-resistant container for their storage. Better yet, create an outside rack for them.

You'll find that large, plastic storage containers provide maximum effective use of the space in your exterior cabinets.

Patio furniture and outdoor cooking equipment will be readily available if stowed on the entry-door side of the RV.

Tools, kept in the trailer's tow vehicle or the motorhome's towee vehicle, will be available when you are driving the transportation vehicle without the RV.

If these vehicles are trucks, you have additional storage space in their beds, especially if they have camper shells.

Finally, when you're packed and ready to go, take your fully-loaded RV to the scales and weigh it again. Front axle, rear axle, side-to-side. Don't forget to weigh the trailer's fully-loaded tow vehicle or the motorhome's fully-loaded towee.

With any luck you'll be within your rig's gross vehicle weight rating.

You can minimize packing and unpacking between trips by permanently storing as much as possible in the RV. Many RVers equip and stock their rigs so they only have to add perishable foods and a few items of clothing before getting on the road.

We maintain a list of the things we routinely pack in our RV. Another list is created for those articles we want to take on that particular journey.

When items are moved into the RV, they are checked off on the list.

So what do we do if we forget to pack something? Anything we forget, we buy along the way or we do without.

When it comes to packing an RV, you might not be able to take all the stuff you want. But, with a little bit of organization and creativity, you should be able to take all the stuff you need.

# Chapter 6

# ON THE ROAD

## Information To Go

Where can I go? What is there to see and do? How do I get there?

One of the keys to successful RVing is knowing how and where to get the answers to these questions.

A variety of information sources are available for avid RVers. Here are a few to get you started.

**Campground and/or RV Park Directory** - A campground directory is a basic RVing necessity. It provides an easy-to-follow system of maps and alphabetical listings which enable you to identify the overnight facilities located in the area you wish to stay.

Each campground listing provides the name, phone number and directions to the campground from the nearest main highway. A description of the campground, its facilities and fees helps you select the one suited to your needs and budget. Finally, a rating system gives you an idea of the quality, completeness and cleanliness of the facilities.

Some campground directories provide additional information such as state highway laws regulating RVs, bridge, tunnel and ferry restrictions and locations of disposal stations along major highways.

Most RVers travel with two or three different campground directories.

**RV Magazines** - Subscribe to at least one RV magazine. You'll be able to read about interesting places to go and things to see and do. How-to articles provide good information on improving, maintaining and repairing your rig. Technical and lifestyle experts respond to reader inquiries. Letters to the editor provide insight into the thoughts, complaints and quandaries of the subscribers.

We recommend you subscribe to both a nationwide and a regional magazine. The nationwide will give you a broad perspective on the issues. The regional will provide you with information about camping destinations and RV services close to home.

**Newspaper and Magazine Travel Sections** - Although they may not be RV specific, many articles will be of interest to the RV traveler. Start saving those articles about places that interest you. We have a file folder for each state that we refer to when we are planning our travels.

**RV Clubs** - Join at least one nationwide RV club. Good Sam RV Owners Club (800-234-3456), Family Motor Coach Association (800-543-3622) and Escapees RV Club (888-SKP-CLUB) are among the largest. These clubs offer insurance programs, emergency roadside services and discounts at campgrounds. Membership also includes a periodic magazine with informative articles and columns. You'll also find the latest in RV books and other sources of information publicized or advertised in these magazines.

Club rallies will feature educational seminars by experts in every RV subject imaginable.

Local RV clubs schedule weekend trips throughout the year. What better way to discover the campgrounds available in your area.

Brand-name RV clubs are excellent sources of RV information and ideas. If you have a question about your RV, chances are that someone in that club who owns a similar model will know the answer.

**Automobile Clubs** - The American Automobile Association, for example, is an excellent source for road maps and tour books. Members may also avail themselves of a trip routing service called Triptic. A Triptic is a series of loosely bound strip maps. They provide detailed information about the road, terrain and points of interest along your chosen route.

**RV Accessory Store or Catalog** - Most RV accessory stores will have a magazine and book rack. RV books not normally found in bookstores will be on display here. RV accessory catalogs offer RVing books and will keep you abreast of the latest in accessories and gadgets.

**Libraries and Bookstores** - It seems obvious, but many people overlook these treasure troves of information. Look under Camping, Motorhomes, Recreation, Recreation Vehicles and Travel Trailers. While you're there look in the library's travel section for information on every state and tourist destination.

**Computer Internet Web Sites** - There are a variety of web sites offering information from RV manufacturers, dealers, campgrounds, clubs and more.

**Computer On-line Services** - Find out which on-line services offer RV forums. RV enthusiasts exchange experience, advice and ideas. RV manufacturers, dealers, service centers and publications participate in "discussions" and help with questions and problems.

**Computer Software Stores** - Mapping and travel software is available for computer owners. RVers can plot their trips based upon the quickest, shortest or most scenic route.

**Government Travel and Camping Information** - Send for information about camping on public lands.

National Park Service
1849 C Street, NW
MS-1013
Washington, DC 20240

National Forest Service
U.S. Department of Agriculture
Office of Information
P.O. Box 96090
Washington, DC 20090

National Wildlife Refuges
U.S. Fish and Wildlife Service
Public Affairs Office
1849 C Street, NW
Washington, DC 20240

Bureau of Land Management
Public Affairs Office
1849 C Street NW
Washington, DC 20240

U.S. Army Corps of Engineers
OCE Publications Depot
2803 52nd Avenue
Hyattsville, MD 20781-1102

Check your campground directory for the address of each state's bureau of tourism. Send to them for state maps, campground directories and travel information.

County Parks and Recreation Departments, located in the county seat, can provide information about their county's camping opportunities.

**Visitor Welcome Centers** - Most states provide a visitor welcome center near their borders. Look for them in rest areas as you cross from one state to the next. Welcome centers will house racks of informative brochures placed there by commercial interests.

After perusing the brochure racks, go to the counter and ask for a state road map, state parks & campground directory and any other specialized information you can't find in the open. Often the best stuff is located behind the counter.

**Travel Plazas (truck stops)** - Travel plazas are courting the business of RV travelers. Some have even installed RV fuel islands for easy access. Visit their convenience store and check out their magazine and book rack. You'll discover that the map and travel information needs of truckers is very similar to those of RVers.

**Campground Stores** - Their magazine, book and brochure racks may have information about RVs, RVing and local places of interest.

**Campground Laundry Rooms** - Here is where you get, firsthand, all the latest and the best information. RVers have a tendency to chat while waiting for their clothes to wash and dry. There's an excellent chance the person sharing the laundry room with you has just come from the direction you're heading. They can tell you their impressions of road conditions, campgrounds and attractions they have encountered. Some of our best tips and money-saving advice has come from people we've met in campground laundry rooms.

## Travel Considerations

The joy of RV travel is that it is different than automobile travel. You don't have to search for a clean public restroom, convenient restaurant or vacant motel. You're traveling with all of the comforts of home. You're traveling first class. Enjoy it!

Plan your RV trips so everyone is comfortable and has a good time. Here are a few considerations:

Take advantage of the "low-occupancy" times. The "shoulder" months consisting of May, June, September and October experience mild weather and less travelers in most of the country. The weekend before a three-day holiday is usually a lot less crowded. Sunday afternoon and Monday morning offer the best opportunity to obtain a desired campsite on a first-come, first-served basis.

Use detailed road maps with time and mileage indicators. Automobile clubs are excellent sources of good maps. Keep in mind that RVs will generally take about ten percent longer than indicated on the map.

Use a highlighter pen to mark your route. When choosing your roads, you may want to avoid the heavy traffic of big cities and the engine strain of steep mountain passes.

Most RV rigs are designed to maintain a highway cruising speed of 55 miles per hour. It's not unusual for RVers to drive faster but generally, at the end of the day, most will have averaged 45 to 50 miles per hour. So, no matter how fast you drive, when planning your travel day figure that you'll average 45 to 50 miles per hour on the main highways.

Many new RVers will drive ten or more hours a day just as they did in an automobile. These impatient folks zoom from destination to destination intent on driving as many miles as possible. They don't see much along the way and are too tired to enjoy much when they reach their destination. This can be particularly grueling when traveling long distances and this pace is repeated day after day.

The majority of seasoned RV travelers have discovered that between four and six hours of driving time each day is a much more comfortable pace. It allows them to stop at interesting spots, enjoy a leisurely lunch and to arrive at their destination in a relaxed frame of mind.

While an occasional long driving day is OK, try to keep your actual driving time to less than six hours per day. It may take some attitude adjusting but you and your family will enjoy your travels a lot more.

Drive during the early hours of the day. Driving into the morning sun is less brutal than driving into the late afternoon sun. Your mind is fresh and clear. You'll avoid the heat of the day and winds will be less of a problem. Driving through hot deserts and mountain passes during the cool early hours of the day is also easier on your rig's engine.

Time your travels to avoid getting caught in commuter traffic. Every major population center has its "rush hour". Expect heavy weekend traffic if you travel on late Friday or Sunday afternoons.

Take a break every couple of hours. Walk your rig. Check underneath (for leaks), look at the tires (for damage), feel the hubs (for excessive heat), shake the trailer hitch and connections (for security).

Your lunch break can occur at a roadside rest area, a restaurant (try a local specialty), a city park (kids can use the playground), or an interesting tourist attraction (factory tours and historical sites are our favorites).

Lunch is also a good time to look ahead and select an overnight camping destination.

Plan on stopping early for the night. RV parks and campgrounds will have more vacancies. You may find a waterfront campsite. There'll be time to go for a walk, take a swim or treat yourself to a nap.

## Locating An RV Park Or Campground

Get a complete RV park and campground directory. You'll find them at book and RV accessory stores. The directories list the RV parks and campgrounds by area. You simply open the book to the area where you want to stay to find the campgrounds available.

Each individual listing will include information about the campground, its facilities and fees. Owners of large rigs should pay particular attention to the campground's size limitations.

Commercial directories don't always list the government campgrounds. Try to obtain listings or directories of the National, State, County and City campgrounds in the areas you are visiting.

Reservations at campgrounds and RV parks should be made according to the location and time of year just as you would at a hotel or motel. If you want to stay on a holiday or summer weekend, reservations might be wise. If you will arrive during the middle of the week or during the off season, reservations may not be necessary.

Many RVers prefer to travel without the constraints of an itinerary. They don't make reservations because they don't know where they will be on any given day. Others, with a particular destination and time frame in mind, will secure their campsite by making reservations. RVing offers this freedom of choice.

Before stopping for the night, refer to your campground directory. Select a couple of RV parks or campgrounds that fit your needs and budget. It's not a bad idea to personally check the facilities, especially the restroom and laundry, before registering. This can be important if you plan to use the showers or wash a load of clothes.

Government campgrounds frequently let you drive through, select an empty site and then return to register. Camping fees are generally the same for all the sites.

RV parks and commercial campgrounds will generally register you and assign you to a campsite immediately upon your arrival. Camping fees will vary according to the hookup facilities you request and, on occasion, the size and location of the site.

Most RV parks and campgrounds post their campsite rates on a board behind the registration desk. There may be a basic overnight fee with additional charges for each hookup service. There may also be additional charges for more than two persons, pets, additional vehicles and use of air conditioners or electric heaters.

Many RVers want full hookups every night and are willing to pay for them, others may only request electric and water hookups. They will use the campground's disposal station when they leave in the morning. Some RVers will ask for just a "dry" campsite.

A lot of RV parks and campgrounds offer discounts to members of RV clubs. Some offer weekly and monthly rates. Inquire about discounts and rates before registering.

Ask for:

A site that will accommodate your slide-out room.

A pull-through site if you have a long rig.

Hookup connections on the left (driver's) side of the campsite. (That's where your RV's connections are located.)

A shady site in the summer (bird and tree sap droppings may come with it).

A sunny site when it's cold.

A site close to the recreational facilities if you won't mind the noise.

A site convenient to the restroom if you won't mind the foot traffic.

A site near the laundry room if you are going to use it.

Look over the literature you are given when you register. It may tell you what channels have which TV networks, what churches, restaurants and stores are in the neighborhood and other local items of interest. Patronize the advertisers on the campground literature, they clearly want your business.

*Tip: Here are some ways you can reduce the cost of overnight camping:*

*Use your campground directory(s) to compare the  prices of campgrounds in the area you wish to spend the night.*

*Take advantage of your RV or auto club discounts.*

*Select and only pay for the utilitiy hookups you need.*

*Ask about weekly or monthly rates.*

*Don't overlook the sometimes less expensive campgrounds in National, State, County and City  parks.*

*And our favorite, cultivate lots of friends with long driveways.*

## Leveling An RV

Before pulling into your campsite, check for hazards and obstacles on the ground, in the air and on both sides of the site. You don't want to drive into a low-hanging wire or partially submerged pipe. See if the hookups you requested are there and are in working order. It would be a shame to back in, level your rig and discover the water is brown.

Leveling an RV is pretty straightforward. It's usually accomplished by rolling the wheel(s) on the lower side of the rig up on top of a board or two. Most RVers use varying lengths of 2 x 6 or 2 x 8 planks for their leveling boards.

Bubble levels, permanently mounted on your rig, will make leveling easier. You'll want two levels, one for side-to-side leveling and the other for front-to-rear.

Leveling boards are not difficult to use. With experience you'll soon be able to quickly gauge how many boards should be placed under a wheel to boost the rig into a level position.

Begin by locating the RV in as level a spot as possible. Next, place an appropriate number of boards in front of the wheel(s) on the lower side of the rig . Finally, drive the wheels on top of the boards.

Level a trailer side-to-side first; block the wheels, then disconnect it from the tow vehicle. Now use the tongue jack to level the trailer front-to-rear.

A motorhome, with wheels on all four corners, may require different numbers of boards under as many as three wheels before it is leveled.

Power levelers are great labor savers, but in some instances, leveling your RV may still require placing boards under a wheel or two. Some power-leveler manufacturers caution against lifting a motorhome's wheel clear of the ground. Ask your dealer about this.

Stabilizing jacks prevent a trailer from bouncing as the occupants move about inside the rig. They are not intended to level and support the weight of an RV.

Once the trailer is level, position the rear stabilizers on the ground about halfway between the axle and the rear bumper. Front stabilizers may be positioned a couple of feet behind the front corners of the RV. Now extend the jacks until they put upward pressure against the main frame rails. Your rig is now leveled and stabilized.

## Connecting To Utility Hookups

Once an RV is parked and leveled, you can turn on the propane and connect to the campground's utility hookups.

After turning on the propane, most experienced RVers hook up the electricity (while the ground is dry), the water next (before they handle the sewer equipment) and the sewer hose last.

**Propane** - Turn on the propane at the tank. Next, turn on the propane-leak detector. You should now be able to ignite and operate all gas-operated appliances.

It's not unususal, after a period of storage, for the propane to have left the lines. It may take up to a minute for propane to flow from the tank to the appliances.

**Electrical hookup** - The electrical hookup is pretty straightforward. One end of the RV's electrical cord is usually permanently attached to the RV. The other end plugs into the campground's electrical outlet.

The RV park's electrical hookup receptacles are generally in a gray box on a post. Most boxes are hinged at the top and open by lifting the front.

There may be breaker switches inside the box. They look and operate pretty much the same as a household light switch. When the switch is down, the electricity to the outlet should be disconnected. When the switch is up, the electric outlet should have power. Move the switches to the "off" position to avoid any chance of a shock while plugging in the RV's electrical cord.

The campground's electric hookup box will usually contain a 20-amp and a 30-amp receptacle. Some will also have a 50-

amp outlet. Each outlet is a different size. The larger in diameter the outlet, the more amps it provides.

If you have a polarity tester, now is the time to plug it into the campground receptacle and check the polarity of the outlet.

Next, plug your cord into the appropriate receptacle. It won't fit any other. If your plug won't fit the available receptacle, you'll have to use an adapter. (See "Equipping Your RV")

Once your RV's electrical cord is plugged in, flip the campground's electrical breaker switch up to the "on" position. All of your RV's electric appliances and outlets should now be operational.

**Water hookup** - The campground's water hookup is a standard water-hose faucet or spigot.

Run the water for a few seconds to wash out any contaminants. Use a paper cup and catch a water sample to view and smell. Don't hook up to a water source that looks or smells bad.

Place your water-pressure regulator on the faucet to protect the hose and the RV plumbing from sudden surges in pressure.

Now, attach your water filter, if you are using one.

Next, attach your water hose. Before connecting the hose to the RV, run water through the hose to eliminate any stale water and air.

Turn off the water and connect the hose to your RV. Turn on the water and check for leaks.

*Tip: Put water-hose quick-connects on your water-pressure regulator, filter and hoses to make the hookup and disconnect process faster and easier.*

**Sewer hookup** - The RV park's sewer inlet is essentially a three to four-inch-wide pipe located at ground level. A screw-in plug with a square tip will probably block the opening.

Remove the sewer-inlet plug and look inside the opening for any obstacles (trash, rocks, etc.).

Using appropriate adapters, first connect the sewer hose to the campground's sewer inlet, then connect the hose to the RV's holding-tank (or sewer) outlet.

At this point, the gray-water valve may be pulled open and left open to allow the shower and sink water to flow immediately into the sewer (we prefer to leave ours closed) .

The black-water valve, though, should remain closed until the black-water tank is about one-third to one-half full. Leaving the black-water valve open may result in a buildup of solid waste in the tank and the valve being clogged with sediment.

*Tip: Consider wearing disposable plastic gloves when handling the sewer equipment. Reusable gloves can become a breeding ground for germs and bacteria.*

**TV antenna hookup** - The campground's TV antenna hookup (if there is one) is frequently located on the same post as the electrical hookup. Simply connect one end of your antenna cable to the campground hookup and the other end of the cable to the RV's cable antenna connection.

**Refrigerator** - Following the manufacturer's instructions, turn on the refrigerator to either propane or electric operation.

## Disconnecting From Hookups

Most experienced RVers disconnect the electricity first (while the ground is dry), the water next (before they handle the sewer equipment) and the sewer hose last.

**TV antenna cable** - Disconnect, coil and store.

**Electrical** - Flip the breaker switches (if any) down to the "off" position. Pull the plug (and adapter), coil the cord and store.

*Tip: Standing at the RV end of the cord and coiling the cord towards you will prevent tangling.*

**Water** - Turn off the water at the campground faucet. Release water pressure by briefly opening and closing a faucet inside the RV. Disconnect the hose from the RV and water pressure regulator. Simultaneously coil and drain the hose. Connect both hose ends together to keep moisture in and insects and dirt out. Disconnect the water filter and store it in a plastic bag to keep it clean. Remove the water-pressure regulator from the spigot and store it where it will remain clean.

**Emptying holding tanks** - Whenever possible, empty the holding tanks before traveling. There's no point in carrying unnecessary weight. The procedure for dumping at a disposal station is the same as when you're connected to a campground's sewer hookup. Wear disposable gloves to protect yourself from bacteria.

*Tip: On most rigs, raising the curb side of the RV by driving up on leveling boards or extending the curb-side leveling jacks will increase the angle of drainage and improve the flushing action.*

Connect the sewer hose to the campground's sewer inlet or place the end of the hose into the disposal station opening. Connect the other end of the hose to the RV's sewer outlet.

Dump the black-water holding tank first. (Take precautions so the hose won't jump out of the sewer inlet when the force of the waste water hits it.) Just pull the valve open. When the black-water tank has stopped draining, lift the hose to completely empty it into the sewer inlet. Close the black-water tank valve by pushing it in.

*Tip: The more liquid there is in the black-water tank before dumping, the better the flushing action. You can add water to the tank by repeatedly flushing the toilet or filling a bucket from the campground's faucet and pouring it into the toilet.*

Now, dump the gray-water tank. Just pull the valve open. The gray water will flush the remaining black water from the RV's sewer outlet and sewer hose. When the gray-water tank has emptied, lift the hose to drain it. Close the gray-water tank valve.

It's not necessary to thoroughly rinse the holding tanks and sewer hose every time you dump. The gray water will generally do a pretty good job of rinsing out the RV's sewer outlet and sewer hose.

Disconnect the sewer hose from the RV and lift it to drain any remaining water into the sewer inlet. Remove the hose from the sewer inlet and store the hose. Replace the sewer inlet plug.

Add a few gallons of water to each holding tank to prevent any remaining waste from solidifying. (The quickest and easiest way to add water to the holding tanks is to fill a bucket from the RV park's faucet and dump it into the RV's toilet and sink. Some prefer to leave the water hookup in place and run water into the sink and toilet.)

*Tip: Periodically, before driving down the road, add five or six gallons of water to each holding tank plus a little liquid soap. When you arrive at your destination, dump both tanks. You have just washed your tanks and sewer hose.*

## Setting Up For Self-contained Camping

Once the RV is leveled and stabilized, be sure both holding-tank valves are pushed in to the closed position.

Turn on the propane at the tank and turn on the propane-leak detector.

Following the manufacturer's instructions, switch the refrigerator to propane operation.

All the 12-volt lights, fans (including the furnace fan) and appliances will draw their power from the coach's deep-cycle battery(s).

Turn the electrical switch for the battery-operated water pump to "on." Now, whenever a faucet is opened, water will flow from the faucets and you will hear the sound of the water pump working. When you turn the faucet off, the pump may continue to run for a second or two before it stops.

The waste water from the sinks and shower will be captured by the gray-water holding tank and the toilet waste will be retained by the black-water holding tank.

Check the monitor panel at least once a day to keep track of the battery's state of charge as well as the levels of the water tank, propane tank and holding tanks.

**Generator operation** - The roof air conditioner(s) and appliances such as microwave oven, toasters and hair dryers will not operate on the 12-volt current provided by the coach battery. When you don't have an electrical hookup, the generator can supply 120-volt (household) electricity to power these items.

Before starting the generator, check to be sure there is adequate clearance between the generator exhaust pipe and any flammable materials such as grass, bushes, etc. Turn off all the 120-volt appliances before starting the generator.

Most generators have a START/STOP button. Press in the "start" side of the button and hold it there until the generator begins to run. Wait one or two minutes for the generator to warm up and reach operating speed before you turn on any appliances.

Close any windows or vents near the generator to prevent its exhaust from entering the RV. Do not go to sleep with the generator running; a carbon monoxide leak could go undetected.

Once a generator is started, it is best to let it run for at least a half an hour and to operate some of the 120-volt appliances before stopping it.

A few minutes before stopping the generator, turn off the 120-volt appliances. This provides the generator a "cooling down" period. Press the "stop" side of the START/STOP button and hold it there until the generator comes to a complete stop.

Do read and comply with the campground's rules about generator operation. Many campgrounds have instituted "generator hours" or prohibit their use altogether. Be considerate of your neighbors. Think about the effect the generator's noise and fumes will have upon them.

## Breaking Camp

**Inside:**

Turn off the appliances (stove, oven, water heater, furnace and water pump).

Turn off the refrigerator. Lock the refrigerator door.

Lower the TV antenna. Close the windows and roof vents.

Check for any forgotten items that should be secured or stored for travel.

Check all cupboards, drawers and closets to be sure they're secured.

**Outside:**

Turn propane off at the tank(s).

Disconnect from the RV park's utility hookups.

Retract the leveling jacks, store the stabilizing jacks, drive off of and store the leveling boards. Don't forget to retract the entry steps!

Before leaving camp is a good time to wash the windshield and to check the engine oil, tire pressure and tightness of wheel-lug nuts. And always check the running lights, turn signals and brake lights.

# Departure Checklist

## Interior:

Store or secure loose items
Turn off:
    Water pump
    Water heater
    Pilot lights (stove and oven)
    Furnace
    Refrigerator (or switch to 12-volt operation)
Secure refrigerator door
Retract TV antenna
Secure cupboards and doors
Close vents and windows
Retract levelers

## Outside:

Check tires and undercarriage
Store personal belongings
Store exterior door mat
Retract awnings
Turn off propane at tank
Store antenna cable
Store electrical cord
Store water hose, filter and pressure regulator
Dump black water then gray water
Store sewer hose
Retrieve and store leveling boards
Hitch up tow vehicle
Lock exterior cabinets
Check brake, signal running and headlights
Retract doorstep
Lock entry door

## Self-contained Camping

You'll discover that while most of the campgrounds in government parks may not offer utility hookups, they do have fresh-water faucets and waste-water disposal stations.

"Roughing it" means using the self-containment features of your rig and taking your RV's water and holding tanks to these facilities when it becomes necessary.

Capacities vary but most RVs will allow you to camp comfortably for at least two to three days without hookups.

You can extend this "dry-camping" time by practicing conservation, expanding the RV's self-containment capabilities or a combination of the two.

There are a number of ways to stretch your self-containment capabilities.

**Conserve water** - Use the campground's restroom and shower facilities whenever possible.

Take a "navy" shower in your RV. Use a minimal amount of water to get wet, turn off the water, soap yourself and then use only enough water to rinse off. Some folks brag about using no more than a gallon of water when they shower this way.

Use the same technique to wash your hands and face.

Don't let the water run while brushing your teeth.

Shave with a rechargeable, battery-operated shaver rather than using a razor and water.

Wash dishes only once a day. Instead of pre-rinsing, use paper towels to wipe leftover food from the dishes.

Conserving water will automatically conserve holding tank space.

**Conserve propane** - Propane lasts a long time. You can make it last even longer by turning on the water heater just once a day to heat water for showers and washing dishes.

It takes only 30 to 40 minutes to heat the tank. Then you can turn it off for the remainder of the day.

You can also save propane by heating enough water in a teakettle to do dishes rather than heating the six to ten gallons of water in your water heater. Light the burner under the kettle when you sit down to eat. The water will be hot by the time you are finished.

**Conserve battery power** - Most new RVs come equipped with a Group 24 deep-cycle battery. This battery has a capacity of about 80 amp-hours of electricity.

A single 12-volt ceiling light bulb draws 1.5 to 2 amps of electricity. The water pump uses about 5 amps when it's in use and the furnace fan draws 7.5 amps while operating.

You can conserve battery power by turning off unnecessary lights. Many 12-volt RV light fixtures come equipped with two bulbs. Will one bulb do the job? Using less water will minimize the amount of battery power consumed by the water pump. Keeping furnace usage to a minimum will also conserve battery capacity.

**Conserve holding tank space** - The gray-water tanks on most RVs rarely have a capacity that equals the capacity of their fresh-water tanks. Black-water tanks, on the other hand, are generally larger than necessary.

When conserving, you can save gray-water tank space by washing dishes in a plastic dishpan and emptying the dishwater into the toilet's black-water tank. We have had occasions when we even captured shower water and dumped it into the black-water tank.

In extreme cases, dishwater can be recycled by saving it (in a bucket or plastic jug) for flushing the toilet. Fortunately, for most of us, measures this extreme are few and far between.

Your RV's self-containment capabilities can be expanded a number of ways.

A generator will provide 120-volt household power and slowly recharge your batteries. Make sure the generator produces sufficient wattage for your needs.

The good news about solar power is, it really works. The bad news is, the equipment can be expensive. It's possible to install a solar system that will operate all of your RV's 120-volt appliances except the air-conditioner.

Fluorescent fixtures use less electricity and provide more light. It's not difficult to replace a standard 12-volt ceiling light fixture with a 12-volt fluorescent one.

Quartz-halogen light bulbs are brighter than the standard 12-volt RV bulbs and use less amperage. They are available with adapters to fit the RV sockets. Since they are expensive, we only use them in our reading lamps.

When it's time to replace the coach battery, buy a Group 27 deep-cycle battery. It will provide 105 amp-hours of electricity versus the Group 24 battery's 80 amp-hours.

Check into the possibility of installing two 6-volt golf-cart batteries in your coach. Wired in series for a 12-volt output, the batteries will supply about 220 amp-hours.

If you are going to camp self-contained in cold weather for any length of time, you might check into the benefits of acquiring a catalytic heater. It will conserve propane as well as the battery powere ectricity it takes to operate the furnace fan.

Our RV has two 6-volt batteries and we avoid cold weather whenever possible (or stay in RV parks with electrical hookups), so we haven't felt the need for a catalytic heater.

A portable holding tank, available at RV accessory stores, can be connected to the RV's sewer outlet to capture gray water. Depending upon their size, these tanks can collect up to 30 gallons. They even have wheels that make it easier to take them to a campground's disposal station.

The self-containment features of your RV are made to order for enjoying our government parks and campgrounds. They can also work well in a friends' long driveway.

We typically prefer to camp self-contained for two or three days and then go to a campground with electric, water and sewer hookups for a day or two. The drive is usually long enough to recharge our coach batteries.

We take advantage of the campground's 120-volt electricity to use our vacuum cleaner, the water hookup to refill our water tank and the sewer hookup to empty our holding tanks.

By the way, even though our RV has a 100-gallon water tank, we rarely travel with more than 30 gallons of water on board. 30 gallons is more than enough to last us two days and that extra 70 gallons of water would mean about 580 pounds of excess weight. If we know we are going to be camping self-contained for any length of time, we fill our tank just before going to our site.

## Cold Weather Camping

Experienced RVers know that the cool weather months can be a great time to camp and travel in an RV. Traffic is lighter, campgrounds have vacancies and the weather is invigorating.

Today's insulated RVs, with their built-in heating systems, provide a cozy retreat from wet weather and nippy air. Soup, coffee or hot chocolate is quickly prepared on the kitchen stove. Comfort lovers can enjoy the luxury of curling up on the couch with a good book while others take advantage of outdoors activities. Clothing to match the changing weather is conveniently available in closets and drawers.

Wherever you go during the fall and winter months, anticipate cold weather. It's the rare RVer who won't be surprised by a sudden drop in air temperature. We were enroute to sunny Mexico one February and ran into freezing temperatures in Tucson, Arizona.

Begin the cold-weather season by lubricating the chassis and changing the oil and oil filter on your engine and generator. Refer to your owner's manual to see what grade of oil is recommended for the anticipated temperature range.

Drain, backflush and refill the engine's cooling system. Ideally, this should be done every year. A 50% water and 50% antifreeze mixture in the radiator should give you protection to 34 degrees below zero. This is also a good time to check the heater hoses and heater operation.

Engines demand more electrical starting power during cold weather. Check the battery's electrolyte level, clean the terminals and coat them with petroleum jelly.

If your vehicle is equipped with an auxiliary transmission cooler, check to be sure your transmission fluid returns directly to the transmission from the radiator's built-in transmission cooler. While this cooler removes heat from the transmission fluid in the summer it also warms the fluid to proper operating temperatures in the winter.

Check the condition of the windshield wiper blades and the operation of the windshield washer. Fill the reservoir with windshield washer fluid. Check to be sure the windshield washer fluid contains methanol and won't freeze.

Buy a set of tire chains if you think you'll encounter snow and ice. Practice putting them on while it's warm and dry. Be sure the chains fit snug and there are no loose ends. You don't want anything beating against the body of your RV as you drive down the road.

Fill the propane tank. This will help prevent vaporization problems in cold temperatures and minimize condensation inside the tank.

Your RV's built-in space heating system should be adequate for keeping the interior warm. Keep in mind, however, that a forced-air furnace will not only consume propane but will draw about 7 amps to operate the furnace fan. This could represent a considerable drain on the coach battery if no hookups are available.

Consider augmenting the propane furnace with a portable electric heater. Although an electric heater requires an electric hookup, it will help reduce consumption of propane. Be sure the RV hookup cord and any extension cord to the heater have a sufficient amperage rating to withstand the wattage of the heater. Divide the heater's maximum wattage by 120 (volts) to determine the minimum amperage rating of the electrical cord. (A 1500 watt heater would require an electrical cord with a minimal rating of 12.5 amps.)

Many RVers who do a lot of self-contained camping use catalytic heaters. Catalytic heaters combine propane and oxygen over a platinum-impregnated pad. The chemical reaction releases energy in the form of radiated heat. It requires no electricity and utilizes propane more efficiently than a forced air-heater.

Most catalytic heaters are not vented to the outside. They consume oxygen from inside the RV and should only be operated when open windows can provide ventilation. A window and a roof vent, each open 6 square inches, should provide adequate ventilation for a 6,000 BTU catalytic heater.

There are also a number of ways to improve an RV's ability to retain heat. Heavy drapes or curtains will insulate the windows against the cold. An insulating dead air space can be created by covering the inside of the windows with clear, heavy vinyl. Some RVers cut sheets of Styrofoam to cover the inside of their windows.

A heavy blanket hung between the driver's compartment and the rest of a motorhome will block the cold radiated by the windshield. Roof vents can be covered on the inside with Styrofoam or snap-on vinyl covers.

Throw rugs, especially on vinyl flooring, will add insulation to the floors. They'll also protect the carpeting against tracked in dirt and moisture.

Weatherstripping around entry doors and exterior cabinet doors will prevent cold drafts.

Styrofoam or fiberglass insulation could be attached to the inside of exterior cabinet doors.

Examine your rig's plumbing to determine what measures may be needed to prevent damage from freezing temperatures.

Some RV manufacturers protect the fresh-water tanks, water pump, pipes, drains, holding tanks and dumping valves by placing them in heated channels and compartments. The heat source is generally the forced-air furnace. As long as the furnace runs periodically, the water in the pipes and tanks shouldn't freeze.

A number of RVs are constructed with the water tank and water pump under a bed or dinette and the pipes inside the kitchen and bath cabinets. The drains, holding tanks and dumping valves, however, may be below the floor and exposed to outside temperatures.

Empty the holding tanks if they will be subject to freezing and pour a couple of quarts of non-toxic, biodegradable antifreeze into each holding tank. This will protect the dump valves. Pour in more antifreeze (1 gallon of anti-freeze to 10 gallons of waste-water should do it) as waste water fills the tanks. Pouring the antifreeze into the gray-water tank through the shower drain will also protect the drain pipe below the shower.

The drinking water and sewer-hookup hoses should be disconnected, emptied and stored when outside temperatures approach freezing. It's also a good idea to slightly open the doors of interior cupboards that contain plumbing. This will allow heated air from the coach to circulate around the pipes.

If you are unable to protect the fresh-water pump or plumbing from freezing, it is best to completely drain the system. Even better protection is provided by using compressed air to blow the remaining water from the pipes or by simply pumping non-toxic, potable antifreeze throughout the water system.

Some cold-weather RVers winterize and then don't use their plumbing system. Instead, they carry containers of drinking water inside the living area of the RV and rely completely upon the campground's restroom facilities. Call ahead if this is your plan. Some campgrounds close their restrooms during the off season and others may only provide electrical hookups.

Electric tank-heating pads and electric heating tape can also be used to protect plumbing when you stay in a campground or RV park with electrical hookups.

Hot water, hair dryers and ordinary electric heating pads are the usual tools for thawing out frozen hoses, pipes and valves.

And more advice: Before driving into an area on a dirt road, consider what it will be like to drive out on that road when it is slick from rain.

Camp in a spot that is open to the heat of the sun and, if possible, protected from the wind. Facing the RV into or away from the prevailing wind will minimize cold drafts.

Keep in mind that snow accumulating on overhanging branches may eventually drop off in heavy clumps or perhaps bring down the brittle branches. Don't let snow block the refrigerator roof vent.

Be sure someone at home knows where you'll be camping.

Cold-weather camping doesn't necessarily have to include freezing temperatures and snow but be prepared for occasional rain and some cold weather. And don't be surprised if you find yourself in an almost empty campground experiencing warm, balmy weather.

Your RV is, in all likelihood, built for a certain amount of cold-weather camping. All you need to add is common sense and perhaps some antifreeze and snow chains. And don't forget the hot chocolate!

# Chapter 7

## AT HOME ON THE ROAD

### Clothing

Take clothing for the weather and activities you anticipate. Most RVers are pretty casual in their dress, so choose clothes you will be comfortable wearing.

Weekenders need only pack the clothes appropriate for their destination and activities. Vacationers may want to add some moderately dressy clothing for flexibility when choosing restaurants. Extended travelers should consider taking clothes for all occasions and weather conditions. One dressy outfit, by the way, is always a good idea for that unexpected wedding or other special occasion.

Take enough clothes for seven to ten days. If you're only going to be gone a week or so, you won't have to worry about doing laundry at all. For longer trips, though, plan on doing laundry about once a week.

Mix-and-match apparel can keep clothing to a minimum. Be sure to take easy-care, durable clothing; commercial washers and dryers are hard on things. Try to minimize the number of articles that will require ironing.

### Laundry

Unless you're lucky enough to have a built-in clothes hamper in your RV, you'll need some type of container for your dirty clothes. A large mesh laundry bag works well. It can be stored in a closet, the shower or an out-of-the-way corner. When the bag gets full, you know it's time to do the laundry!

Most commercial RV parks and many campgrounds have laundry rooms with coin-operated washers and dryers. Some are even equipped with change machines and soap dispensers.

If you will be ironing clothes while traveling, you'll be happy to know that many of the RV parks have started putting ironing boards in laundry rooms. They may even loan you an iron but you'll probably want to carry your own, just in case.

Not only are campground laundry rooms convenient for washing clothes, you'll find they're also great places to exchange travel information with other RVers.

Some campground laundry rooms are better equipped than others. If doing laundry the night of your arrival is important to you, it might be wise to check the facilities before registering. You can go on to another campground if the facilities, equipment or cleanliness are not acceptable.

You'll find commercial laundromats everywhere you go. Even the smallest towns have them. Some even have showers.

Try to find a laundromat located in a shopping center with a food market.  You'll be able to do your laundry and food shopping in one stop.

Many commercial laundromats will do your laundry for you. There is a charge, but it just might be worth it to you.  Drop off your clothes and go sightseeing. At the end of the day you can pick up the clean, folded clothes and you're on your way.

Here are some tips for making laundry day easy while traveling:

Save quarters to use in the washers and dryers.  A 35mm film canister will hold $7.00 worth of quarters very conveniently. We always carry several full canisters, just in case.

Be prepared. Have your own laundry supplies and don't be dependent upon their availability at campground stores or in vending machines.

Buy small or medium-size containers of laundry supplies. Those large economy-size boxes and jugs are difficult to store and awkward to carry.

Use a detergent that works in cold water. Hot water may not be available.

Always check the insides of washers and dryers before using them. You never know what someone might have left in there.

It's always a good idea to clean the dryer's lint filter . That will make a big difference in the time required for drying.

Folks with a washer and dryer in their rig find that doing one load a day is the best way to keep up with the laundry. Knowing it's going to take time, they start a load as soon as they are hooked up at the campground.

## Meal Preparation and Cleanup

Some RVers never use their RV kitchens. They eat all their meals in restaurants. Others fix three complete meals every day. Most of us fall somewhere in between.

It's not unusual for weekenders to prepare the weekend's main meals at home during the week. The meals are frozen or refrigerated and campground meal preparation is simply a matter of reheating.

Most RVers do a lot of outdoor cooking. The food is easy to prepare, always seems to taste better and cleanup is a breeze.

Extended travelers, after they've been on the road for a while, get hungry for "home-made" meals and tend to use their RV kitchens as often as they do at home.

You'll find that you can prepare just about anything once you are comfortable with your RV kitchen.

Here are some suggestions for making life easier in the RV galley:

Use Teflon pans and skillets.

Line baking pans with aluminum foil.

Use disposable plates, bowls and cups whenever possible.

Wipe off dishes and pans with paper towels before washing them. It's the rare RV, today, that has a garbage disposal.

Use plastic trash-can liners. Food, scraps, grease and coffee grounds can be thrown directly in the trash.

And, of course, you can always eat out more often.

## Housekeeping

"A place for everything and everything in its place." "Neatness counts." Those phrases must have been coined by an RVer. A jacket thrown on the couch or a toy left on the floor will make the RV seem cluttered and start the walls closing in on you.

Clean as you go. There's really not much to clean. Wait until you return from the weekend or the one-week vacation to thoroughly clean and vacuum. On longer trips, choose a "housekeeping" day to change the sheets, vacuum the floor and scrub the bathroom.

Some seasoned RVers set aside a morning once a week to do the laundry, clean the RV and shop for groceries. They get it all done and use only a half day to do it.

## Telephone Communications

We happen to be among those who think that not having a telephone is one of the joys of RV ownership. There are times, though, when using a telephone is a necessity. Fortunately, there are a number of telecommunication tools available to the RV traveler.

**Public Telephones** are available almost everywhere you go. You can place a call by inserting coins or calling collect.

**Calling Cards** are a more convenient way to place calls at a public telephone. You can get one from your local telephone service provider or from a long-distance carrier such as AT&T, MCI or Sprint.

There is no monthly service fee for a calling card but a surcharge may be added for each call you place using the card. This surcharge could amount to two or three times the cost of a local call, so keep some coins handy for local calls.

Don't let anyone see or hear you using your calling card number. If they are able to copy it, they may be able to place calls that will show up on your telephone bill.

*Tip: Always dial the access number for your long-distance carrier before placing a long-distance call. Some local phone companies have been known to levy unusually high long-distance charges at their phone booths.*

**Prepaid Phone Cards** can save you money. The cards can be purchased in denominations of $5, $10, $20 and more. You'll find them for sale in department stores, supermarkets and drug stores. Be sure you buy from a reputable source. There are some fraudulent prepaid phone cards out there.

One big advantage to the prepaid phone card is that, since the card is paid for at the time of purchase, you will not receive a phone bill for long-distance calls.

Here's how the prepaid phone card works: When you purchase the card, you buy a given amount of telephone calling time. Usually, the higher the denomination of the card, the less you are paying for each  minute of calling time. A $5 prepaid calling card, for example, may provide you with 20 minutes of calling time. That figures out to 25 cents for each minute of calling time. A $50 card, on the other hand, may provide 250 minutes of calling time at 20 cents a minute.

When you use a prepaid phone card, it doesn't matter what time, what day or what place in the USA you are calling. The per-minute charge is the same. This can be an economical advantage to RV travelers who wish to place long-distance calls during the daytime hours.

Check to see if the card has an expiration date. You don't want to buy a card with more telephone calling time than you'll be able to use.

**Answering Machines** allow people to leave messages for you at home. You can retrieve and respond to those messages while you're on the road.

These handy devices should be purchased with the following features:

One, "remote," will enable you to listen to your messages while you are away from home.

The other, "tollsaver," can save you the price of a toll call if there are no messages on your answering machine.

The "tollsaver" feature allows you to program the answering machine to answer the phone on the first ring if there are any messages but to wait until the fourth ring if there are not any messages.

When you call for messages and your home phone rings more than one time, you can assume there are no messages, hang up before the answering machine answers the phone on the fourth ring and save yourself the cost of a toll call.

Incidentally, don't invite any burglars by announcing on your answering machine that you are on vacation.

**Voice Mail Service** may be offered by your local telephone company. This service is similar to an answering machine except the equipment is owned and operated by telephone company. The phone company doesn't offer any kind of "tollsaver" feature in conjunction with its voice-mail service.

**Emergency Telephone Message Service** is offered to the members of some RV and automobile travel clubs as a benefit of membership. Typically, the caller dials an 800 number to leave an emergency message and the member dials an 800 number to retrieve the message. A service like this can be worth the price of a club's annual membership.

**Commercial Voice Mail Services** advertise in RV magazines. Many of the RV clubs offer some form of message service for a moderate fee.

**Cellular Telephones** allow you to place or receive telephone calls in nearly all populated areas and along most major highways throughout the USA and Canada.

RV travelers with cellular phones feel secure knowing they can call for help in an emergency. They also have peace of mind knowing their families can reach them if there is an emergency at home.

Cellular service charges, however, can mount up quickly. In addition to a monthly service fee, be prepared to pay for each minute of phone usage (airtime) for both incoming and outgoing calls.

When you leave your "home" cellular company's area and travel into the geographical area of another cellular company, you become a "roamer". The cellular calls you place or receive are now relayed by the host area's local cellular company.

Cellular calls placed or received by "roamers" are subject to the charges of the host area's local cellular company. Generally, a "roamer's" fee, ranging from three to six dollars, is charged once on any day a cellular call is placed or received. Additionally, a "roamer" can also expect to be charged in the neighborhood of a dollar a minute for airtime.

As you can see, your "home" cellular company's agreement only applies while you are in your "home" area. "Roamers" pay what the host area's cellular company wants to charge them.

"Roamers" expect to pay long-distance charges when they place a long-distance call. They may be surprised, however, when they are billed for incoming long-distance calls.

When callers dial your cellular phone number, they are only charged for the standard telephone calls to your "home" cellular area. You are charged for the long-distance calls from your "home" cellular area to your present location.

You can control your cellular costs by limiting the number of cellular calls, both incoming and outgoing, and the amount of time spent on the cellular phone.

Since you pay for all incoming calls, you may want to limit the number of people who know your cellular phone number.

Consider starting out with the cellular company's economy plan and with only one or two close family members knowing your cellular number. Later, if you want a more expensive plan, the cellular company should be happy to oblige and you can always add to the list of those who have your number.

Your personal circumstances and budget will dictate how you handle your own telephone communications.

We have found the calling card, answering machine, and a cellular phone (economy plan and used only for emergencies) have been more than adequate for our extended RV travel needs.

## Receiving Mail

It's not difficult to receive mail while on the road. First, identify a friend or relative who is willing to retrieve the mail from your mail box at home and forward it to you. Tell them you will call periodically, identify those pieces of mail you want forwarded and let them know where it should be sent.

You can receive your mail at post offices along your travel route by having it sent to you in care of General Delivery. All your mail should be put into a single envelope and addressed to you as follows:

>John & Mary Traveler
>
>c/o General Delivery
>
>City, State, Zip Code

When we are being sent a lot of mail, our forwarder uses Priority Mail. The post office provides a large cardboard Priority Mail envelope. Our mail forwarder can stuff the envelope full and send it for the two-pound postage rate (even if it weighs more). Priority Mail frequently arrives in two days and rarely takes more than four.

The receiving post office will hold general delivery mail for you for 10 days and then return it to the sender. Some may hold your mail a little longer if you call or write.

Be sure to choose a small town to receive your mail. The advantage is that you, the tourist, will find it easier to locate the post office. Ask anyone in a small town and they'll be able to direct you to the post office. You're also more likely to find room to park your RV when you go to a small town post office.

*Tip: Get a Zip Code Directory. Small towns will have only one zip code. Multiple zip codes may indicate several post office branches within the city.*

You may be able to have your mail forwarded to you in care of an RV park. Before having it sent there, however, ask the park management for permission and find out what their procedures are for receiving and holding your mail.

Fulltime RVers and those considering going on the road for extended periods of time can utilize professional mail forwarding services. You'll find them advertised in the RV magazines. The larger RV clubs also offer dependable mail forwarding service at a nominal fee.

## Cash On The Road

Today's electronic technology allows RVers to obtain cash at banks all over the country. Here are a few thoughts about obtaining cash and making purchases while on the road.

**Cash** - There's an old adage, "Don't carry more cash than you can afford to lose." The availability of ATMs and credit cards eliminates the necessity of carrying large amounts of cash on your person.  Determine the amount of cash you will require. Hide or secure some of it in your rig and divide the rest between you and your traveling partner.

**Traveler's Checks** - Traveler's checks are the next best thing to cash.

They may be used to obtain local currency while you are in Canada or Mexico and many RVers carry them as an "emergency cash fund."

Traveler's checks are easy to cash at financial institutions. You'll find that supermarkets and restaurants are also convenient places to cash a traveler's check.  Just make a purchase, pay for it with a traveler's check and receive change.

Many financial institutions, automobile and travel clubs offer their account holders and members fee-free traveler's checks.

**Personal Checks** - Many merchants are wary of accepting out-of-town checks and banks make it difficult to write a check for cash.  You'll find, however,  there are a lot of RV parks and campgrounds that will accept out-of-town personal checks.

In any case, you'll want to take along your checkbook to pay bills (such as your credit card balance) by mail.

**ATM Cards** - The advent of the ATM has made it easy for the RVer to obtain cash almost anywhere while traveling.

When you use your ATM card to get cash, the amount is immediately withdrawn from your checking or savings account.

As an RV traveler, you will want your ATM and credit cards affiliated with at least one of the ATM networks that provide nationwide ATM access. MasterCard's Cirrus and Visa's Plus are two such networks and, in fact, are international in scope. If your card bears either of their logos, you can use it at any affiliated ATM in the USA or abroad.

Keep in mind you may be charged a transaction fee for each ATM withdrawal. Many financial institutions, however, don't charge their customers a fee for withdrawals made from their own network. There may be an advantage to establishing your account with a bank that boasts a large or interstate branch network.

**Credit Cards** - Most merchants, including RV parks, campgrounds and service stations, accept credit cards. Major cards like MasterCard and Visa are readily accepted in Canada and automatically give you a decent rate of exchange.

**Wire Transfer** - Don't overlook companies like Western Union if you want to send or receive large amounts of cash quickly. The process is as simple as the sender handing the wire-transfer agent the cash (and a money transfer fee); the money is available to the recipient within minutes.

Keep it simple. Minimize your need for cash by using a check or credit card for as many purchases as possible. Use an ATM to obtain additional cash. Don't carry any more cash than necessary.

## Banking and Bill Paying

RVers who spend more than a few weeks on the road eventually have to find a way to deal with their banking and bill-paying responsibilities.

One method is to have all your statements and bills forwarded to you by mail, then pay them as you do at home. Another is to estimate and prepay your bills for the period you'll be on the road.

A preferred alternative is to develop a simplified banking and bill paying system that will make life easier for you both at home and on the road.

You can simplify your banking needs by consolidating all your accounts at one financial institution. Check out the services offered by banks, savings and loans, credit unions and brokerage houses. You probably won't need a personal relationship with your banker, so choose a financial institution that offers:

Free or low cost services

Interest earning checking and savings accounts.

Overdraft or automatic advance on checking accounts.

ATM card associated with a large ATM network such as Cirrus, Plus or Star.

Visa or MasterCard.

Debit card.

Electronic deposit of income from regular income sources.

Automatic electronic payment of mortgages, loans, utilities, etc.

Telephone banking and transfer services.

Bank by mail service.

Telephone bill-paying service (800 number; you dictate payments).

Availability of safe-deposit boxes for documents and valuables.

Minimize your need to go to the bank by:

Electronically depositing income.

Using the bank's telephone banking and transfer service.

Banking by mail.

Minimize the number and expense of writing and mailing checks by:

Electronically paying as many regular bills as possible (loans, utilities, etc.).

Using the bank's telephone bill-paying service.

Minimize the amount of cash you need to carry by:

Using your credit card and/or writing checks instead of paying cash.

Using your ATM card to obtain cash as you travel.

Minimize the number of statements and bills you receive in the mail and the number of checks you have to write by using only one credit card (MasterCard or Visa for example).

Pay the credit card balance before interest charges are levied.

Rather than wait for your monthly credit card statement to be forwarded, you can add up the credit card receipts you have generated while on the road and write a check for the amount due.

You can also call the Customer Service 800 number on the back of your credit card, find out your balance and write a check to pay it off.

Your objective should be to minimize the time, effort and expense associated with banking and bill paying.

If you can handle these transactions at home with two or three pieces of mail or a couple of phone calls, you can do the same while on the road.

Obviously, consolidating or minimizing your bills will make this chore a lot easier.

## Medical Considerations

Good medical care is available just about anywhere your RV travels take you.

If you are under the regular care of a physicain, ask for a copy of your medical records to take with you. These copies may save valuable time (and money) if you need to see a doctor while on the road.

You should aso check with your HMO or medical insurer to see what procedures you should follow when obtaining medical care on the road. Generally, you are covered wherever you go if you follow their guidelines.

Should you have a health problem while you're traveling, consider these alternatives:

If it's a real emergency, go to a hospital emergency room. Keep in mind that if it's not that urgent, you'll have to wait while the real emergencies are treated. There's also the likelihood that you'll pay more for that treatment in an emergency room than you would at a doctor's office.

Doctors offices are usually located in the immediate neighborhood of a hospital. Pick one out, walk in and arrange payment up front (most will accept a credit card). If they tell you they are not taking new patients, let them know you are just traveling through and don't want to establish yourself as a regular patient.

Go to a walk-in medical clinic. They advertise in the yellow pages and are located everywhere. We have received excellent treatment in these facilities all over the country.

Ask the campground operator or manager to recommend a doctor or medical facility. Chances are they'll point you in the direction of their own doctor.

Don't assume you will be able to walk into a drugstore in another state and get your prescription (re)filled. Most prescriptions can only be filled in the state in which they are written.

Before leaving on an extended RV trip, ask your physician to prescribe a sufficient quantity of medication or refills to last until you return home.

Then, if possible, take enough of the medication with you to last the duration of your trip. (Check with your pharmacist, but most medication will do well if stored in a cool, dark location in your RV.)

If your pharmacist will not fill large quantities of your medication at a time, here are some alternatives:

Fill your initial prescription at a pharmacy convenient to the person who will be forwarding your mail. Perhaps they can get your refills and send them to you with your mail.

Look into mail-order pharmacies. AARP is one that comes to mind. Their prices are very reasonable and they can mail prescriptions to your travel location.

Some RV travelers get their initial prescription filled at a pharmacy in a nationwide chain such as K-Mart or Wal-Mart. They are usually able to get a refill at another pharmacy in that chain even though it's located in a different state.

An important point here. Don't make any assumptions. Check with the pharmacist first. Will your friend be permitted to obtain your refills? Can the mail-order pharmacy send your prescriptions to the states you will be visiting? Will you be able to get your prescription refilled (and how often) at the pharmacy chain in the states you travel through?

By the way, don't overlook the obvious. Find out if your local pharmacist will refill and mail your prescriptions to you.

## RVing With Dogs and Cats

A lot of RVers take their dogs and cats on the road. Some of these pets, like human beings, readily adapt and even look forward to RV travel while others have difficulty adjusting.

Keep in mind the animal will be barraged by new sights, sounds and smells. They will have strangers in close proximity. This can be stressful for some and could cause barking (in dogs) and unpredictable behavior.

Most, but not all, RV parks and government campgrounds accept dogs and cats. Don't be surprised, however, if there is an extra charge for your pet. You may even be assigned to an area of the campground designated for pet owners.

The campground will ask you to clean up after your pet, keep it on a leash and not allow it to disturb your neighbors. RV pet owners who think these rules do not apply to them are the reason some RV parks and campgrounds now refuse to allow pets.

Carry a valid rabies vaccination certificate if you travel with a dog or cat. Many government campgrounds and some RV parks require them. RVers traveling to and from Canada and Mexico are required to have a valid veterinarian health certificate, including a proof of rabies vaccination.

Be prepared for your dog or cat to get away from you. Put an identification collar on it. Include your RV's make and license number as well as your RV's cellular phone number. Your veterinarian can advise you about identification tattoos and under-the-skin implants. Check into the lost pet service offered by both the Good Sam and the Escapees RV Clubs.

Carry a leash for exercising and some type of tethering rope or chain to keep your pet within the confines of your campsite.

By the way, don't leave your animal unattended outside the RV. It could either attack or be attacked by other animals.

Take care of your animal's health. Mosquitoes transmit heartworm. Ticks and fleas abound in outdoor areas. Ask your veterinarian about preventatives.

Be aware that strange food and water could cause digestive upset. This is not the time to alter your pet's diet.

Think about what you will do with your pet when you are not able to take it with you for the day. You don't want to leave it unattended in a hot or unventilated RV. A vent fan or air-conditioner can be left running, but what if there is a power failure?

Some campgrounds and recreation destinations offer kennels. Ask what protective measures they take against parasites, infection and distemper.

A protective travel case will prevent your pet from becoming a flying missile when the brakes are suddenly applied. It will also keep the animal from interfering with the driver. The travel case can double as a familiar and secure place for your pet to sleep.

Try to locate a permanent place in the RV for the animal's food and water bowls.

Pet odors can build rapidly in the confined space of an RV. You'll want to work diligently to minimize odors and to prevent fleas.

Finally, be a good neighbor. Clean up your pet's waste. Keep it on a leash. And please, don't permit it to bark, whine or otherwise disturb the RVers around you.

## Personal Security

Enjoying your RV is not without risks. RVers can be victims of crime just like anyone else. But when you are RVing you're in a relatively low-crime neighborhood.

There are a number of logical reasons for this.

The activities and attractions that appeal to RVers are not usually located in high-crime areas.

Most RV parks and campgrounds are located on the outskirts of cities and towns. A bothersome commute for most criminals.

RVers generally park in close proximity to other RVers. There always seems to be at least one person sitting outside who seems interested in everything that's going on around them. Non-campers are pretty easy to spot and, as a result, attract attention.

And you never know when a ranger, camp host or strolling camper will pass by. These are people who could come to an RVer's aid or act as witnesses. Criminals prefer to avoid the inconvenience involved with getting caught.

It's difficult to establish patterns of movement or occupancy in and around RVs. We come and go unpredictably.

It's also not easy to determine who or what may be inside an RV. It could be a lineman for the Rams, a Great Dane or a little old lady with a big new gun. Criminals have the same aversion to pain as everyone else.

An RV can be more difficult to break into than a house. (Those of us who have managed to lock ourselves out of an RV can attest to this.) And it certainly can't be done inconspicuously. Again, that getting caught thing.

Finally, there's a notion that all RVers carry guns and are willing to use them.

Essentially, the criminal is an opportunist looking for an easy target, a quick grab and a fast getaway. RVers and their lifestyle generally do not present this kind of opportunity.

Common sense precautions should be taken while RVing just as they are at home. Lock all your doors while driving. Exterior doors, windows and storage lockers should always be locked when not in use.

Hitch locks on trailers are an inexpensive theft deterrent. Don't leave anything outside overnight or while you're absent unless it's secured to the RV, picnic table or a tree with a lock and chain.

Avoid tempting thieves by not displaying cash, cameras, computers, cellular phones or other possessions.

Along the same lines, keep cash, jewelry and other valuables secured and hidden inside the RV.

A dog can be a good theft deterrent, so can a burglar alarm. Some RVers install additional exterior lights.

Over the years, we've met many women traveling alone in their RVs. They are, definitely, among the most creative RVers, especially when it comes to deterring would-be intruders.

One evening, after sharing our campfire with a woman traveling alone, we watched as she returned to her rig. Before she went inside, she opened an outside cupboard and pulled out a huge dog dish. Then came a very large collar attached to a hefty chain. She set the dog dish on the ground, attached the chain to her step, turned around and waved goodnight.

Can you imagine the would-be intruder targeting that RV and then seeing all that paraphernalia obviously belonging to a huge dog? Especially when he realized the dog wasn't controlled by a collar? And is the dog inside or outside?

There's a lot of discussion these days about carrying a gun in an RV. The purpose of a gun is to kill. If you're not prepared to take someone's life, perhaps you should think twice about carrying a gun.

Police officers receive hours and hours of professional training in the use of deadly force. And they occasionally make fatal mistakes. If you do decide to carry a gun, please take a thorough training course in how and when to use it. More importantly, learn when <u>not</u> to use it. After all, we might be parked next door to you some night.

By the way, if you decide to carry a firearm in your RV, familiarize yourself with the gun laws of the cities, counties, states and countries you plan on visiting.

Generally speaking, the RV world is a low-crime neighborhood. RVers are not usually perceived as easy targets of opportunity. Use common sense and you'll minimize the risks of becoming a crime victim.

## Membership Campgrounds

RVers join membership campgrounds for a variety of reasons. The camaraderie of belonging to a group, the feeling of being in a secure environment and the assurance of being able to find a campsite are just a few.

The question of whether to buy into a membership campground, though, should be approached with the same caution as any other serious financial commitment. Investigate before you invest.

Covenants and conditions differ among the various membership campground organizations, but here is a very simplified explanation of how many of them work:

When you join a membership campground you become entitled to camp free in that campground, which we'll refer to as a "home campground," for a specified number of days each year.

You are not purchasing a lot or campsite, only the right, as a member, to use that "home campground."

To join, you pay an initiation (or joining) fee, perhaps in the thousands of dollars. You also commit yourself to paying dues or maintenance fees of possibly a few hundred dollars each year. By the way, it is only realistic to expect the annual dues to increase periodically.

The cost of joining may also include finance charges and miscellaneous costs.

If the "home campground" is associated with other membership campgrounds, you may be able to stay in any of that association's campgrounds, usually for a camping fee of a few of dollars per day.

This "association" privilege may involve an additional initiation fee and slight increase in your annual dues.

Some membership campground associations have an affiliation with other membership campground associations. For an additional joining fee and additional annual dues you may be able to stay in any of the affiliated association's campgrounds. Again, the daily camping fee will probably be nominal.

The appeal of membership campgrounds to many RVers is the ability to camp in a large number of campgrounds for a low daily camping fee.

If that's your reason for joining, you'll want to be sure the affiliated membership campgrounds will be available to you.

There may be a requirement that in order for you to use an affiliated campground or receive the low daily rate, it has to be located a certain distance, perhaps a hundred miles or more, from your "home campground."

Some RVers buy into a "home campground" located in a distant, remote location so they are able to use the various affiliated campgrounds closer to home.

Check to be sure there are affiliated membership campgrounds along the roads you will travel and in the areas you are likely to visit. There's no point in belonging to a membership campground if you're not going to be staying in their campgrounds.

Do some math if your objective in joining a membership campground is to reduce your camping expenses. Figure out how many nights you will have to stay in membership campgrounds, as opposed to non-membership campgrounds, to really save money.

Prices vary but let's say, for example, the initiation (joining fee) in a national affiliation of membership campgrounds costs about $6,000 and the current annual dues are $300 per year. Let's also assume you will use the membership for ten years.

The initiation fee ($6,000) divided by 10 years would amount to $600 per year. The annual dues would add another $300 per year. Using these figures, it would cost $900 per year to maintain a campground membership.

Let's also say a non-membership campground charges about $20 per night for an equivalent campsite. Dividing this $20 into the $900 annual cost of campground membership means you could stay in non-membership campgrounds for 45 nights each year for what it would cost to belong to a membership campground.

This computation does not take into consideration the interest you would have to pay to finance the $6,000 initiation fee or the interest the $6,000 would earn if it remained in your bank account. Nor does it reflect the possibility of assessments and periodic increases in annual dues. It also ignores the probability of increased overnight camping fees at both membership and non-membership campgrounds.

But it does give you a formula to determine if belonging to a membership campground would make financial sense to you.

In this case, if you think that during the next ten years you will spend more than 45 nights per year in membership campgrounds, it might make good financial sense to purchase a membership.

There's also a possibility (but no guarantee) that you could sell your membership at the end of the ten-year period. That would further reduce the overall cost of membership.

Look at the classified section of RV magazines under "Membership Campground Resales" to get an idea of what people are *asking* for their memberships. Resale competition can be pretty keen.

Check out a number of competing membership campgrounds before buying. Visit, or better yet, spend a couple nights in what would be your "home campground." Talk to the members. Ask them if they would recommend joining. Do they have any difficulty making reservations? What is the financial condition of the campground?

Listen to the sales presentations. Ask questions. Take notes.

Ask what the ratio is of members to campsites at the "home campground" you are considering joining. Are non-members, in addition to members of affiliated associations, allowed to camp in your "home campground?" Will campsites be readily available in your "home campground?" Will it be difficult for you to make reservations in the affiliated membership campgrounds?

Find out if you would be allowed to sell your membership during the first few years of ownership. Are there transfer fees or other costs involved in selling your membership? How many times may the membership be resold?

Can your membership be passed on in your estate? What happens if your heirs don't want the membership?

How do you cancel your membership? What are the financial and legal ramifications if you stop paying the annual dues?

What happens to your membership in the affiliated campgrounds and associations if your "home campground" goes bankrupt?

Take home, scrutinize and compare the literature and copies of the contracts.

Consider having a real estate attorney review the contract before signing.

Joining a membership campground should compliment your RVing needs, make financial sense and enhance your enjoyment of RVing.

Investigate before you invest.

# Chapter 8

## CARE AND MAINTENANCE

Your new RV should come with its own care and maintenance manuals. We recommend that, as soon as possible, you also obtain and read an RV repair and maintenance manual. You'll find them in RV accessory stores and catalogs.

Keep in mind your RV is doing heavy duty. The drive componants will require more frequent inspection and maintenance.

Check the engine oil level and examine your tires at the end of each day's travel.

Check the tire pressure once a month, more often if you are traveling every day.

Check the water level in the batteries periodically. Notice if any kind of corrosive deposit is beginning to form near the posts.

Change the engine oil and oil filter every 3,000 miles.

Change the engine coolant every year or 15,000 miles.

Change the transmission fluid and filter at least every 25,000 miles

Clean and lubricate wheel bearings every 25,000 miles.

Inspect the belts and hoses periodically and replace them every five years or 50,000 miles.

Check the oil level in the generator after every 6 to 8 hours of operation

Clean the generator's air filter every 50 hours and replace after 100 hours.

Change the oil in the generator every 100 hours or once a year. Replace the oil and fuel filters at the same time. This is also a good time to replace the spark plug(s).

Examine the caulking on the roof seams and around air conditioners and roof vents. Deteriorated caulking should be replaced.

Clean the exterior as often as necessary. Wash the roof first and the walls immediately afterward.

The front of an RV accumulates a lot of dead bugs. We wash off each day's collection of carcasses with a long handled, soft bristled brush dipped in plain cold water.

## Storing Your RV

Storing an RV between trips involves more than just parking it in an out-of-the-way spot. A few preventive maintenance steps will protect your rig and make it easier to take out on the next trip. Use the following information to develop your own storage procedure and check-list.

Today's RVs, with their electronic appliances and "goodies," are tempting targets for thieves. Choose a storage yard that offers limited access and good security.

Try to store the RV in a spot where it will be protected as much as possible from the elements. Avoid overhead wires and branches that may result in bird droppings or sap. Parking on a slope will encourage water to run off the roof. Make a habit of checking your rig every month or so.

**To store an RV when you <u>don't</u> anticipate freezing temperatures:**

Change the engine oil and oil filter. Combustion by-products mixed with the crankcase oil will etch the bearings if allowed to sit for long periods of time. Run the engine for a few minutes to circulate the new oil. This also applies to the generator's engine.

Obviously, it doesn't make sense to change the oil after every trip. The amount of miles or time since the last oil change and the length of time the RV will be in storage before the next trip will have to be taken into consideration.

Be sure the batteries are fully charged before putting the RV into storage. Storing a partially-charged battery will eventually limit the battery's ability to accept and hold future charges.

Disconnect the battery cables. Clean the terminals and coat them with petroleum jelly to inhibit corrosion. Batteries will self-discharge over a period of time so recharge them every month or so.

Fill the fuel tank to minimize condensation. Add a can of fuel stabilizer (available at auto parts stores) if the RV is going to be stored for more then a couple of months. Diesel owners should treat their fuel with an algicide. Run the engine and generator to get the treated fuel into the fuel lines and carburetors.

Note: Diesel owners should refer to their owner's manual or ask their dealer's advice for the blend of fuel and any fuel additives recommended for their anticipated storage time and temperatures.

Cover the tires to protect them from the sun, ultraviolet rays and ozone.

Inspect the roof and, if necessary, recaulk the seams. Recaulking the roof seams to prevent leaks is something that should be done every two or three years.

Clean the awning. Be sure it is completely dry before rolling it up.

Clean the exterior of the RV. Polish or wax the exterior at least once a year.

Cover the roof air conditioner(s).

Some people also cover the furnace air inlets and outlets and the water heater and refrigerator wall vents to discourage insects from setting up housekeeping.

*Tip: Spiders are attracted by the smell of propane. Their webs can interfere with the propane operation of the refrigerator. Place a few mothballs in the refrigerator's exterior compartment to discourage them. The same applies to the propane water heater.*

A lightweight, opaque polyester cover will protect the exterior finish from sun damage.

Defrost and clean the refrigerator. Store it with the doors propped open to prevent mold and mildew. An open box of baking soda will prevent odors.

Clean the interior of the RV.

Close the drapes to prevent sun damage to the interior.

Turn off all propane appliances.

Turn off all electrical appliances and devices.

Remove batteries from clocks, flashlights, portable radios, etc. to guard against corrosion damage.

A roof vent cover will allow you to crack open the bathroom vent to allow a little ventilation.

Turn off the propane at the tank. A full propane tank will minimize condensation.

Dump, clean and rinse holding tanks. Close the valves and cover the opening with the cap. Add a few gallons of water to the tanks. This will keep the seals moist and prevent any remaining waste from drying and adhering to the tank floors.

Drain all the water from the fresh-water tank. Check the owner's manual or ask your dealer for the location of the drain valves.

Note: As an emergency preparedness measure, we prefer to store our RV with the water tank full. We add a teaspoon of household bleach for every ten gallons of water in the tank. The stored water is replaced with fresh water prior to taking the rig on a trip.

Putting the rig back in service amounts to little more than reconnecting the battery cables, removing the protective covers and filling the water tank.

## When freezing temperatures <u>are</u> anticipated:

Drain, backflush and replenish the cooling system with a 50-50 mixture of water and antifreeze. This will give you protection to 34 degrees below zero.

Remove and store the batteries in a cool (but above freezing), dry place. A battery without a full charge can freeze and become permanently damaged. Recharge the batteries every month or so.

Remove food and liquids that could freeze if left inside the RV.

Drain all the liquid from the holding tanks

Drain all the water from the fresh-water tank.

Drain the water heater. Opening the pressure relief valve and/or hot-water faucets will permit air to enter the tank and allow the water to drain faster.

Open any water drains your rig may have. When the water has stopped draining, open all the faucets and turn on the water pump. Let it run until no more water appears. Turn off the water pump, close the drain valves and shut off the faucets.

You now have your choice of either blowing the remaining water out of the system with compressed air or replacing the water with a non-toxic antifreeze.

**Blowing the water out** costs less and doesn't leave a funny aftertaste. There is, however, the possibility that a small amount of water will remain in the system, eventually collect at the lowest point and freeze.

You'll need a blow-out plug. This device allows you to connect an air hose to the RV's city-water hookup inlet so you can blow the remaining water from the system. You can make a blow-out plug but they are relatively inexpensive at an RV accessory store.

Connect the blow-out plug to the city water inlet on your RV. Be sure there's a filter on the air output side of the air compressor to prevent contamination of your rig's water system.

Note: Generally, tire pumps and small compressors don't build up enough pressure to adequately clear the water from the system.

The best method for blowing out the water lines is to have one person outside the RV operating the air hose and another person inside the rig opening and closing the faucets. The idea is to always have at least one faucet open to prevent the air pressure from rupturing the plumbing.

Now open and close every faucet, one at a time, to blow out the remaining water. Begin with the hot and cold water faucets furthest from the water pump. Allow a blast of air to blow through each faucet for about 15 to 20 seconds. Be sure to include the ice maker, washing machine and outside shower. Operate the toilet's flushing mechanism to blow out any water.

Remove the water pressure source and store the rig with the faucets open.

**Protecting the plumbing with non-toxic antifreeze** may be simpler than blowing the water out. If you select the non-toxic antifreeze method, close all the faucets and drain valves after the water is drained.

Close the appropriate valves on your hot-water heater's bypass to disconnect it from the rest of the water system. If it is not equipped with a bypass, you can buy one at your RV accessory store or have a service technician install one. Without a hot-water heater bypass you'll need an additional six to ten gallons of non-toxic antifreeze (depending upon the volume of your water heater). A water heater bypass will usually cost less than six gallons of non-toxic antifreeze.

Use a non-toxic, potable antifreeze designed for use in fresh drinking-water systems. It may be purchased at RV accessory stores. Automotive antifreeze is poisonous and could damage the PVC plumbing and/or the seals in the holding tank valves.

Note: non-toxic potable antifreeze (propylene glycol) is light red or pink while automotive antifreeze (ethylene glycol) is green or blue. Always be sure to read the label before adding antifreeze to your water system.

Pour three to five gallons of non-toxic antifreeze into the fresh-water tank. Add more non-toxic antifreeze only if your water pump begins to run dry before completing the following steps.

*Tip: Some RV water tanks might take a couple of gallons of antifreeze before the antifreeze is available to the water pump. Save the expense of that antifreeze by disconnecting the hose between the water tank outlet and the water pump inlet. Now connect one end of a hose to the inlet side of the water pump and put the other end in the antifreeze container. The water pump can now pump antifreeze directly from the container and into the plumbing. The water tank does not have to be stored with antifreeze in it if the tank has been thoroughly drained.*

Turn on the water pump. Beginning with the faucets furthest from the pump, open each of them, one at a time, until antifreeze appears at the spout. Allow about a cup of antifreeze to drain into the sink and shower drain traps to prevent them from freezing. Operate the toilet flushing mechanism until a small amount of antifreeze is in the bottom of the bowl. Turn off the pump and store the rig with the faucets open.

Read the instructions on your water filter/purifier about winter storage. If you leave the cartridge in when you put antifreeze in the system, be sure to replace it with a new one when you take the rig out of storage.

If your rig is equipped with a clothes washing machine, run antifreeze through the hot and cold water lines. Pour a gallon of antifreeze into the washing machine. Then turn the timer to "spin" to pump out the antifreeze. Next, go back to "fill" and add about half a gallon. Pump this out again. This will ensure that the water pump and discharge lines have adequate antifreeze.

Pour RV non-toxic antifreeze into the holding tanks to protect the valves.

**Getting your RV back in service:** If you used the blow-out method, all you need to do is close all the faucets, connect to a city water hookup and run water through all the faucets to evacuate the air.

If you used non-toxic antifreeze, drain all the antifreeze from the water tank, pipes and water heater (cooking antifreeze in the water heater could damage it). You can collect the antifreeze and use it again next year.

Fill the fresh-water tank about one-third to one-half full with fresh water. Turn on the water pump and open one faucet at a time (including the toilet flushing mechanism) until all the antifreeze has run out of the lines.

Now drain the fresh-water tank. Refill the water tank and repeat the above steps to thoroughly flush the antifreeze out of the water system.

## If the rig is going to be stored for longer than three or four months:

Coat the upper cylinder and valve area of both the automotive and generator engines by slowly pouring a few ounces of light oil into the air intake downstream of the air filter while the engine is idling. Turn off the engine when smoke appears at the exhaust.

Remove the spark plugs on both the automotive and the generator engines and inject a few squirts of oil through the openings. Before reconnecting the spark plug wires, crank the engines a few times to distribute the oil throughout the cylinders. Replace the spark plugs.

Experts seem to agree it is best to <u>not</u> run the engine for short periods of time while the rig is in storage. If the engine is started, drive the rig for ten or more miles at highway speeds to remove moisture and harmful chemicals from the crankcase.

Support the vehicle on blocks (not the leveling jacks) and reduce tire pressure by 10 to 20 pounds per square inch.

Seal or cover all openings (refrigerator, water heater, furnace, kitchen fan, roof vents) against moisture, dust, insects and small animals. Heavy plastic sheeting or aluminum foil should do the job.

Remove the batteries and store them, fully charged, in a cool (but above freezing), dry place. Recharge the batteries every month or so.

To put the rig back in service: Re-install the batteries, re-inflate the tires and remove the support blocks. Remove the covers from the refrigerator, water heater, furnace, kitchen fan and roof vents.

The engine(s) may be slow to restart. Fuel has to reach the engine. Oil in the cylinders may result in a smoky exhaust and rough operation until the oil is burned off.

Life is short.

Whatever your destination,

Whichever route you choose,

Enjoy The Journey!

*Joe & Vicki Kieva*